# Offshore
## or
# DIE!

Award-Winning Chartered Accountant reveals
how to solve all of your accounting firm's
staffing issues with an offshore team

MARK COTTLE
WITH JON RYALL

**Offshore or DIE!**

# TESTIMONIALS

**Paul Hawksley**
TWP Accounting - Partner
www. twpaccounting.co.uk

*Like other firms, we had been unsuccessful with outsourcing and were slow to learn the difference between it and offshoring. Right from my initial communications with Mark, I found him to be honest about what can be achieved and the potential hurdles that need to be overcome. He also offered expert advice on how to meet these challenges. It is refreshing to deal with someone who is open and honest and tells it how it is without any pretence.*

*We have been using Frontline for the past six months and have been extremely impressed with the quality of the staff recruited to join our team. The HR team are great at weeding out unsuitable candidates and only the strongest ones are put forward.*

*Having visited the Frontline office in Manila, it was great to get a feel for the atmosphere. All the members of staff were extremely motivated, keen to help and professional. The office environment is one of the best I have seen in any accountancy firm.*

*Our original idea was to use the team for routine low-level processing. However, we are constantly finding that they have far more capability and are keen to learn more.*

*We are now at a point where we are reaping the benefits of the offshore team and would like to thank Mark and his team for working with us to achieve a successful solution.*

# TESTIMONIALS

**Jon Baggott**
Numeric Accounting - Director
www. numericaccounting.co.uk

*I first met Mark at a conference around April 2015 and I was intrigued by the concept of staff leasing. We were already using a traditional outsourcing model, which did an okay job, but we had some quality control issues. We also had no control over the staff or job timings. Mark gave me a copy of the first edition of 'Offshore or Die!' to read (which I did!), but I was unsure about the idea and we shelved it for a while.*

*We met again at another conference later that year. In the meantime, we had been recruiting in the UK in the normal way but had found there was a serious shortage of quality candidates and had been unable to fill the roles. So we decided it was time to give Mark's offshoring model a try.*

*The recruitment process was amazingly thorough, unlike anything we had experienced in the UK...and it cost a lot less too. As a result, we ended up with the most fantastic employee who has been a real star and a great addition to our team.*

*Since then we have recruited a second employee through Frontline and the experience has been very similar to the first. Our small 'team' works closely together, which improves their efficiency. Their work ethic is excellent and our Filipino staff members are also fun to work with.*

*Frontline continue to deliver a well-managed, professional service for us and I would have no hesitation recommending Mark and his team to any other firms who are forward-thinking enough to give offshoring a try.*

# TESTIMONIALS

**Malcolm Palmer**

A4G - Managing Partner

www.a4g-llp.co.uk

*We've been offshoring work for 12 years now and for most of that time we used a completely unreliable supplier in India.*

*We met Mark in November 2015 and we now have nine members of staff working in the Philippines.*

*Having the huge pool of talent available to recruit via Mark's company has been a godsend to us. Frontline has never over promised and usually over delivers. As a result, we have some great members of staff working for us.*

*In circumstances where we have lost one or two weaker members of staff in the UK through natural wastage, we have recruited excellent replacements in the Philippines via Mark. As a result, our senior staff and managers have had the capacity to spend more time with clients.*

# TESTIMONIALS

**Nadi Elias**

Equus Partners – CEO
www.equuspartners.com.au

*After undertaking a study tour of the BPO industry in June 2014 and meeting with a number of reputable suppliers, we engaged Frontline as our key supplier in the Philippines.*

*Being an Australian accounting and financial services firm, it was of utmost importance that we selected an organisation who not only supplied accounting staff to the Australian market but who specifically recruited, trained, developed and culturally familiarised accountants for Australian accounting firms. Frontline have so far impressed us in the following three ways:*

*1. Recruitment – I was fortunate to sit in on a few random interviews with Mark at our first meeting. Immediately, Mark and his team were able to demonstrate their ability to execute a recruitment style which endeavoured to hire loyal, hardworking, intelligent accountants with outstanding personalities. When it was our time to interview, we were confident the shortlisted candidates were going to be a good fit. It was of no surprise to us that the process was seamless.*

*2. Training – Mark and his team exceeded our expectations by providing initial guidance to us (as first-timers) and furthermore by providing training programmes to our team to bring them up to speed with Australian tax legislation and regulation.*

*3. Culture – A true understanding of the culture at Frontline was cemented after my first team-training trip to Manila in September 2014. It didn't take long for me to get a sense of family, unity and fun. This is a testament to the way Mark builds a firm culture that rewards hard work and promotes team spirit.*

# TESTIMONIALS

*In addition to the above, Mark's understanding of the industry, the local environment, the people and our business has allowed him to become more of a partner than a supplier. We have constantly thrown curve ball questions at Mark and his team, only to receive clear and consultative responses.*

*Mark and his team have been outstanding and we look forward to growing our operations through Frontline in the near future.*

**Robert Renting**

RJ Renting & Co. – Director

www.rjrco.com.au

*Making the first move to find out more about Mark's offshoring operation in Manila has turned out to be a good step for the bottom line of my business.*

*Jonathan Ryall was my first contact at Frontline and I was referred onto his partner, Mark Cottle. I can speak very highly of their service and professionalism. Mark has a very good knowledge of the Philippine culture and spent time imparting that information to me prior to the interview with my first employee. He was very helpful and efficient with the selection and interview process and organised interviews with suitably qualified candidates.*

*As the trend for the future appears to be towards overseas offshoring for accounting, I commend Mark and Jonathan on their foresight and courage in setting up what is a trendsetting business model.*

*I have no hesitation in recommending Frontline to any forward-thinking accounting firms and wish them well for what looks to be a good future.*

# TESTIMONIALS

**John Murphy**

Connole Carlisle – Managing Director
www.connolecarlisle.com.au

*I met Mark and his Manila team in January 2014 and was immediately impressed. I can recall reporting to my partners that unless a significantly more impressive BPO firm was put in front of me, we would be using his services.*

*What impressed me most was Mark's 'can do' attitude and how easy it was to communicate with him. Other similar providers in Manila and elsewhere seemed to be far more rigid and wanted to push their virtues through glossy brochures, which didn't impress me. Mark's easy-going, casual (but professional) attitude and demeanour will win him many more clients going forward.*

*When we met, Mark's BPO team comprised 10 members and I've personally watched it grow to beyond 200. I had predicted that Mark's BPO would grow exponentially, which it now clearly has.*

*Mark's outreach work in the Philippines also made an impression. Supporting these needy families is very rewarding and some of the photos Mark showed me of people's living conditions were heart-wrenching. Hopefully, time constraints won't prevent him from continuing with this important work.*

# TESTIMONIALS

## Sean Limpens

BCV Financial Services – Partner
www.bcvfs.com.au

*Having been on a BPO tour of Manila late in 2013, I had little doubt there were some fantastic opportunities for accounting firms looking to offshore work. However, I was a little uncertain about which model to use, as there were advantages and disadvantages to many of them.*

*It was only after an initial meeting with Mark and Jon from Frontline Accounting that I felt I had finally discovered a model that would meet our needs, which included great assistance in sourcing and recruiting staff and an Australian presence in the Manila office, which helped to build our trust. There was also a degree of supervision for our team and continual suggestions and advice on how to induct and train our new team members.*

*Frontline delivered on every promise they made in the initial discussions. Mark and Jon run a very transparent operation and are happy to offer advice as needed. They go over and above in regard to building a 'team within a team' culture. This benefits our staff members and, in turn, our firm. They have made our initial offshoring experience relatively pain-free, and thanks to their help we have a team performing at a level that has exceeded our initial expectations.*

*Frontline has taken it upon themselves to run team-building trips for the staff of all the firms in their office, and they have also organised team tax training sessions to improve everyone's knowledge.*

*The feedback from our team members to date has been fantastic, with all of them lauding the work environment that Frontline has created. I already envisage the need for more staff in the medium term, and have little doubt that Frontline will be able to continue to assist us in developing our offshore presence with their personable and innovative approach.*

# TESTIMONIALS

**Scott Norrish**

Maxim Accounting – Director
www.maximaccounting.com.au

*We've had the pleasure of dealing with Mark, Cherry and the Frontline team since we visited the Philippines in January 2014 looking for new opportunities to expand capacity in our accounting practice. As part of an organised tour, we visited many different service providers (some great, some scary) before we eventually settled with Frontline.*

*We found Mark to be refreshingly upfront and honest (i.e. blunt) and always willing to assist, which is something paramount to the success of any SME considering any sort of offshoring. Also, their accounting practice shares many of our values, characteristics and visions.*

*We wouldn't hesitate to recommend Mark and Frontline Accounting as a service provider to other firms willing to open their minds to a new way of doing business, allowing them to leverage off the opportunities the Philippines provides to enhance the productivity and efficiency of their business model.*

# TESTIMONIALS

**Mark Tinworth**

Tinworth & Co. – Principal
www.tinworthaccountants.com.au

*Mark's casual and relaxed style is the real Aussie deal in Manila and it's a pleasant and refreshing change to the hard grind of business. He tells it how he sees it.*

*As a North Sydney-based firm of Chartered Accountants, we are committed to delivering quality outcomes to our clients. Mark and his team mirror the same level of personal commitment.*

*Ultimately, Mark's business model is a winner for us. His approach to recruiting people of exceptional quality and fostering a professional environment is consistent with our own, and we are really proud of our small team in Manila, which we see as merely an extension of our North Sydney office.*

# TESTIMONIALS

**Rob Byrnes**

Pocket Bookkeeping – Managing Director
www.pocket.com.au

*We chose Frontline after a process of evaluating a wide range of suppliers. There were three key factors that stood out with Frontline and these made them a clear winner in the selection process.*

*Firstly, they specialise in their area of expertise: the accounting market. This has delivered us clear benefits and differentiates Frontline from generic service providers. The advantages include high-quality recruitment that ensures you get the right people for the job and great training and support that includes Xero certification and tax training. Mark has created an environment that feels like a professional Australian accounting practice. It replicates our onshore partners and meets our needs perfectly.*

*Secondly, Mark has a deep understanding of what drives a great culture in an organisation. He has created a great team environment that is both professional and happy. The team look after each other and their clients, and there is a strong sense of loyalty. This is critical to success when establishing small teams in the highly competitive Manila market.*

*Thirdly, Mark is very customer-focused and is based in Manila full-time. He knows what the customer wants, he knows where the team is at and he makes sure the two meet. Having Mark based in Manila full-time does make a significant difference.*

*If you are in the accounting business and are looking for an offshore partner, you won't do better than Frontline.*

# TESTIMONIALS

**Peter Marmara-Stewart**

Preston COE & Ring – Managing Director
www.prestoncoering.com.au

*I came across Frontline through the Proactive Accountants Network. It was evident from my initial conversation with Mark that we were on the same page.*

*Mark spent time explaining via Skype how Frontline's staff leasing model worked for offshoring. It was a thorough discussion, and all my questions were answered. Frontline have been in Manila for some time and know the ropes there.*

*We then went through the process of hiring three employees: two accountants and one admin assistant. Our team has demonstrated their aptitude, desire to learn and the value they will bring to our practice.*

*I would recommend Frontline's model for any firm wanting to free up capacity and improve their bottom line.*

# TESTIMONIALS

**Barclay Judge**

Judge Accountants – Director
www.judgeaccountants.com.au

*Using Frontline Accounting was the best decision I have made in my business.*

*My initial decision to use them was to save labour costs and to allow me to easily scale my staff for our growing firm. However, it has been much better than I initially envisaged.*

*We train our Philippine staff to work with our processes and knowledge base, and their constant motivation, enthusiasm and dedication towards their career makes them fast learners and some of the best employees I have ever had.*

*The Philippine staff members are proudly part of our team, just as our staff in Australia are. The Frontline Accounting team do a brilliant job of taking care of all the office administration and payroll, and they also suggest training programmes to support our staff and make it a fun and rewarding culture for them.*

*Whenever I've had concerns or wanted to increase my staff base in the Philippines, the Frontline Accounting team have been very prompt and on the ball.*

# TESTIMONIALS

## Mo Yusuff

Club Row Creations - Director
www.clubrowcreations.co.uk

*It took me around six months to finally push the button and it was one of the best decisions I've made for a long time.*

*When I first spoke to Mark about taking on an admin person, I was convinced it would be a huge asset to my business. I knew that the people Mark finds all work in his offices in Manila so they operate in a structured, almost corporate (but in a good way) environment.*

*Now, I deliberated for a long time for two reasons.*

*Firstly, I wasn't sure if I'd have enough work for them. In fact, I wasn't sure exactly what I wanted them to do.*

*And secondly, I didn't know how, or even if, I'd be able to train them to do some of the more complicated tasks I had in mind.*

*So after the initial chat on Skype, I told Mark the qualities I was looking for in my new member of staff. These included being able to speak and write English fluently, be an experienced user of MS Office and be able to use their initiative. Oh, and just for good measure, I said that copywriting skills would be an advantage.*

*Now, at this stage I didn't have a specific job role in mind other than they would be helping to add products to the website and doing some of the time-consuming admin jobs. And so Mark went off and got things started. He said it usually took about three weeks to interview and find suitable candidates. Mark has this system where all applicants are required to jump through a few hoops just to be able to get to the interview stage, so anyone he puts forward has been thoroughly assessed.*

*Sure enough, three weeks later, Mark's HR girl sent me CVs and completed interview questionnaires for three applicants. One candidate stood out head and shoulders above the rest. We set up a Skype interview a few days later, loved what we saw and made her an immediate job offer, which she accepted.*

*Dianne started about a week later.*

*I decided to start her off with something fairly simple, which involved logging into my old autoresponder system and transferring a few email campaigns into Google Drive.*

*This should take a day or so to do, I thought. I was wrong. Dianne had completed the task in just a few short hours. OK, so now it was time to transfer those email campaigns into my new autoresponder system, which was not so straightforward. It involved creating a template for each email and playing around with the html code before adding each one to the campaign (one campaign alone contained 30 emails). This'll keep her busy for a couple of days at least, I thought.*

*She completed this task in one day.*

*I found the best way to show Dianne fairly complex tasks was to shoot small training videos of me actually doing the task - and it worked a treat. She simply watches the video a couple of times and she's trained.*

*Five months later, Dianne has added over 500 products to our website, which includes contacting the suppliers for details, adding various filters, general product research and completing descriptions, which usually states what the products do and their benefits. She adds colour options by choosing hex codes, product images and logos if required (we've trained her on Photoshop so she can do this).*

*Other regular tasks she's now responsible for include:*

*Posting my weekly blog and LinkedIn posts, which sometimes means rewriting the first paragraph.*

# TESTIMONIALS

*Looking after my LinkedIn campaigns, sending out emails and managing my LinkedIn group.*

*Looking after my weekly Twitter feeds.*

*We gave her a little training on this and now I don't need to get involved at all.*

*I'm currently training her to do my monthly marketing campaigns, which will include building the webpage, creating the email and follow-up campaign and writing a short sales letter.*

*She'll be doing most of my newsletter from next month too.*

*So, from an initial five or six hours a week of training, I now spend less than two hours a week with Dianne. I've since taken on a second employee and I'm looking to hire a third in the next few months.*

*I would highly recommend Mark and his team and I'm more than happy to discuss my experience with anyone who feels they would benefit from his services.*

# TESTIMONIALS

**Leanne Tunbridge**

Positive Outlook – Director
www.outlookaccounting.com.au

*Positive Outlook Accounting and Business joined Frontline after doing an organised tour and viewing dozens of BPOs in the Philippines.*

*We started with the appointment of two employees in November 2015. Appointing employees in the Philippines has been a journey in understanding their education, needs and culture. It is an investment as the initial learning curve on both sides has been steep. Great communication has been essential to this success.*

*Frontline has been very responsive about ensuring the well-being of my Philippine staff and is proactive about communicating and advising us in this management process. The staff members in Australia are in daily communication and we are a united team.*

# TESTIMONIALS

**Mitch Griffiths**

Rapsey Griffiths – Partner
www.rapseygriffiths.com.au

*Like many firms looking at offshoring, we spent significant time and resources exploring our options and various providers. An existing Frontline client originally referred us to Mark and his team. From our first meeting with Mark we appreciated the upfront and honest advice in relation to what it takes to utilise offshore staffing successfully.*

*Once we signed up with Frontline it was all systems go and the recruitment process was hassle-free. The Frontline staff made the interview process easy for someone who had not had the experience of interviewing offshore-based staff. Mark even attended my staff interviews!*

*Mark and his team provide guidance on all HR and operational issues and really bridge the gap between our Australian-based firm and our offshore workforce. Requests for info on any issues or queries are replied to promptly.*

*I believe that Frontline Accounting is different from a number of other providers because they are using the offshoring model in their own accounting firm. They therefore understand the process and can provide tips along the way.*

*The use of offshore staff has enabled us to manage our capacity issues and has also allowed our Australian-based staff to concentrate on more value added tasks.*

*I highly recommend Frontline's offshoring service.*

# TESTIMONIALS

**Paul Franks**

Lambourne Partners - Partner
www.lambourne.com.au

*I first met Mark and the Frontline team when we were on a tour and visited many offshoring providers. They stood out in terms of their training, location, family environment, atmosphere and attention to detail.*

*Mark and his team have been pioneers in Philippines offshoring. They have recruited for us high-quality, skilled accounting staff. The training programmes that our newly recruited staff undertook with Frontline provided them with excellent practical skills that enabled them to be productive straight after training.*

*Mark consistently provided us with excellent service, was responsive when challenges arose and kept in communication at all times. This gave us confidence that our team would be a success.*

*Having an offshore workforce has allowed our firm to provide additional services to clients, turn around our workflow faster and build a stronger overall team. Most importantly, Mark cares about his staff, our business growth and building a strong and successful offshore team. Any progressive firm should have an offshore division as part of their accounting business. For our firm, offshoring was not about cost reductions, it was about better service for our Australian clients.*

# TESTIMONIALS

## Marc Loader CA GAICD
Verve Group - Director
www.vervegroup.com.au

*Verve Group has been in a partnership with Frontline for over two years. I use the word partnership instead of client because that is how it feels with Mark and his team. They are truly our PH partners.*

*Through Frontline, we have been able to grow our business knowing there will always be the resources we need to deliver to our clients.*

*In our time with Frontline, they have helped us recruit seven employees that are now an integral asset of Verve Group.*

*Frontline's professional attitude means that the process of recruiting, training and supporting our staff is fantastic. My team of seven are seen as much more than just employees.*

*I think the support Mark and the team at Frontline provide is a real shining light for the industry, both here in Australia and in the Philippines. They really care about their people and have shown time and time again how they are there to help, nurture and grow the people that come in through their doors.*

*Without a doubt, it is people first and that is why I will always support Frontline.*

# TESTIMONIALS

**Nikki Adams**

Ad Valorem -Director
www.advaloremgroup.uk

*In common with most practices that specialise in the SME market, several years ago Ad Valorem hit a ceiling of what we were able to charge for basic compliance work. We have always valued our team and getting new business has never been our issue. However, it became clear that the only way we would be able to continue to grow and keep up with our younger, career-driven apprentices/juniors was to look at reducing the costs of producing the more basic sets of accounts, payroll and bookkeeping.*

*We tried outsourcing, as this was being endlessly plugged at accountancy conferences as the answer to our prayers. However, the outsourcing model didn't sit well with us. The relationships we have with our clients and team is built on trust. The client trusts us to do our job properly, keep them legal and provide practical and valuable business advice. The team trusts us to lead the practice through the maelstrom of political and professional constraints whilst providing interesting and exciting opportunities for their future and identifying profitable areas of growth...no wonder so many accountants have nervous breakdowns!*

*It seemed to us that by outsourcing all we were doing was taking away the opportunities for our children's generation and attempting to hoodwink the Ad Valorem clients. In addition, by focusing on the short-term problem, it seemed we were also taking away the future of the practice because eventually the salaries overseas would catch up and our clients would be off dealing with them and not us, as by that time there would be a shortage of good people in the UK. We also didn't see how this would provide job satisfaction for the overseas workers either, as there would be no regular contact with the clients or us. It is a logical model, not a people-orientated model. In the SME market, our belief is that we MUST have a people-orientated model to get the buy-in from our team and clients.*

*When we met Mark Cottle from Frontline at a 2020 Group Annual Conference, we were somewhat sceptical and were ready to write him off as another evangelical offering the answer to our prayers. However, we quickly changed our minds when it became apparent that we shared the same core values and that he is people-focused and not out to make a quick buck. The offshoring model took away the negative feelings we had towards outsourcing. We have taken the plunge and a new manager of our Philippines operation (as we see it) starts tomorrow! The big difference to us is that the worker is dedicated to us and yet is not left to their own devices, having the benefit of being part of Mark's team too.*

*This model gives us the opportunity to offer our price-sensitive clients another choice. It also gives those clients that are growing quickly the chance to use their precious working capital for the high-level advisory work they desperately need but often can't afford in the early days.*

*This way we can afford to reinvest in training apprentices in the UK and give them a career path without always focusing on the dreaded timesheet. Reducing the cost of producing compliance work means our client managers have more time to have those important conversations with their clients – which they never seem to be able to do while they are busy getting the work done.*

*It means we can develop Ad Valorem internationally whilst providing work for less fortunate countries…why wouldn't we do that? It's a win-win!*

### Peter

*Pete, you have made me a proud dad.*
*You are miles ahead of where I was at your age.*

*Keep learning, stay humble and never lose your unstoppable work ethic. It will set you apart from 99% of other people.*


### Cherry

*Cherry, you have supported me through crazy business growth over the last few years.*

*Thanks for your help. I appreciate every minute you've put into the business.*

*And most of all, thanks for putting up with me, and my numerous flaws.*

# CONTENTS

# CONTENTS

# CONTENTS

# FOREWORD(S)

*Author's note:* *Most books have one foreword. I do most things differently, so I have chosen to have two. Most readers of this book live in the UK and Australia. Most accountants in Australia will recognise* **Rob Nixon** *and most accountants in the UK will recognise* **Paul Dunn.** *Rob and Paul are pioneers in the accounting industry, and it's only fitting their comments should appear in my book.*

*******

## Rob Nixon

Dear Accountant,

Since May 1994, I've been advising accountants all over the world on how to run a more efficient accounting firm and deliver value-added services to clients.

In 2011, I discovered 'offshoring' in the Philippines. A friend of mine went on a study tour and was blown away by the possibilities. After hearing him rave about the abundance of people, the cost and the work ethic, I also went on a tour and was equally blown away by the opportunities presented by offshoring.

On the first day of the tour, whilst visiting a BPO (Business Processing Outsourcing), I asked a company official the following question, *"So what can you guys do over here?"*

The answer blew me away.

*"We can do any task that is done over the phone or behind a computer for a 1/3 to a 10th of the cost, often faster and often better."*

WOW. I started writing down tasks in my business and the list was long. I was hooked. I sent some of my team across and we started hiring people. Fast forward a few years and I currently have 26 full-time employees (more than half of our team) in the Philippines. They do all sorts of roles, such as accounting, marketing, sales, administration, software development and client support. They are operating on shifts supporting our team members and our accounting firms in Australia, the UK and the USA.

Think about the answer to this question. *How much of a typical accountant's day is spent behind a computer or over the phone?* You know the answer. Most of it.

These are tasks that can be done for three, four, five or up to ten times less the labour costs!

What an opportunity to solve the age-old problem of 'finding good quality people'. In the world of offshoring, there are thousands of good-quality, hardworking, diligent people who want to work for accounting firms.

This strategy is not about making your current team redundant. It's a growth strategy. There is an abundance of people available with many wide and varied skills that you can hire quickly to help you grow your business.

Although not a redundancy strategy, I do give a word of warning to accountants. And this is:

If you are not adding value to the data that is in front of you on your screens, then your days are numbered!

Either the computer itself will do the data processing or an offshore worker will gladly do the task for three to eight times less salary.

The accounting profession is changing *quickly and dramatically.* Technology is automating many tasks that humans used to do. Accountants MUST add value, add value and add more value. And you must look for ways to reduce your costs.

There are new nimble, tech savvy accounting firms appearing *all* the time. They are low cost and mobile. They can offer a cheaper compliance product and they are. They're automating functions and they're using offshore labour.

I think the future of the accounting profession involves client facing on sales, service and advisory. Anything that is 'back office' or processing can (and should in my view) be done offshore. It just makes commercial sense.

If you are at all interested in this opportunity, then devour Mark's book and then jump on a plane and go and see it with your own eyes. I am sure you'll be equally blown away, just like the hundreds of accountants that are already successfully offshoring were.

This is a massive opportunity for accountants. The only question is, *will you take the leap?*

**Rob Nixon**
*CEO & Founder – PANALITIX*
*Brisbane, Australia*

*www.panalitix.com*
*www.robnixon.com*

Author of 'Accounting Practices Don't Add Up – Why they don't and what to do about it' and 'Remaining Relevant – The future of the accounting profession.'

## Paul Dunn

There has never, *ever* been a time like this.

And that's almost an understatement.

Consider this: in the time it took you to say the word 'time' (about one second), the following things happened:

→ 7,156 Tweets were sent

→ 2,036 Skype calls were made

→ 53,520 Google searches were performed

→ 119,587 YouTube videos were downloaded

→ 2,447,505 Emails were sent

→ 33,894 Gbytes of data came at us

It's staggering. Every relentless second after every second.

And if those numbers blew your mind, check out more at www.internetlivestats.com - you'll be amazed. They capture precisely why this book is so important, as they neatly and powerfully describe not just the all-pervasive disruption, but the staggering speed with which it occurs.

But we need to be *very* clear. It's not technology that causes the disruption, it's the new business models it enables us to create. It's NOT, as so many people think, the tools: this piece of software or that new, faster piece of technology.

For example, people believe they're innovating because they move to cloud technology. Not true. The innovation comes only when they move to embrace the new business models it makes possible. Innovation only comes when people let go of outmoded business structures and beliefs and move to new ways of building businesses.

And, as this book's provocative title so succinctly points out, the alternative to *not* embracing the change is the death of existing models. And the rate of the demise increases each and every day.

We need to let go of long-held beliefs and business models that are, in the case of the accounting profession, centuries old. They bind us to the past.

This book does the opposite. It unleashes a **powerful, positive** and **growing** future.

Follow Mark's journey. It's a **great read**.

But don't simply read, *embrace* what he's experienced and use the processes he's created. You'll love every minute of it.

**Paul Dunn**
*Co-Founder & Chairman - B1G1*
*London, UK*
*www.b1g1.com*

# INTRODUCTION

I do what you do.

*Accounting.*

I run a small Chartered Accounting firm in Melbourne, Australia with my friend and business partner, Jon Ryall.

We produce our work differently to most other firms. Since we launched in 2011, we've built our firm using an offshore model. Much to the envy of many firms I speak to, we have never had local staff. Our team are all based in the Philippines.

This fact alone makes us very unusual. Being unusual also means we haven't faced the same problems that other firms do.

**The biggest problem facing firms right now...**

Most firms struggle *right now* with one primary problem.

**Capacity.**

More specifically, most firms I speak to in Australia and the UK are unable to *find and keep enough good staff*. (We've never had that problem because our model doesn't rely on finding staff in our own backyard.)

It doesn't matter whether the firm is based in Central Sydney or London, or even in a village in the middle of the UK. The problem is the same. And it is the single **biggest source of pain** for the partners of these firms.

Some firms are growing quickly and can't find enough good staff to get the work out the door. Some are in an area where there simply aren't any candidates due to a small population. I speak to firms who have been running recruitment ads for many months and *still* can't fill a basic accounting role.

The good news is that by using an offshore team in the Philippines, this pain is eliminated. Most firms who take the plunge are stoked with the results. It's not uncommon for the offshore staff to do a better job than the locally trained workforce...but I'll discuss that in more depth later.

A secondary issue many firms face is **cost**. It costs a small fortune to hire and train accountants in Australia and the UK. Again, we've never faced that problem because our staff members are all based in a country where wages and the cost of living are a magnitude lower than in Australia and the UK.

We use a model that is still in development. It's not a typical 'outsourcing' one. I'm going to compare and contrast various models for getting work done offshore later in the book. But for now, put aside any preconceived ideas of how offshoring works.

When we started, hardly anyone knew how our offshoring model worked. Now, several years into the journey, more and more firms are learning about what we do and are joining us. But I can assure you that most firms *still* haven't heard of the model we use to get work done offshore.

If our firm is considered an innovator (I guess we are, given we won an award for innovation), most of the firms we work with would be considered early adopters. That leaves the majority who aren't even aware yet of what's going on when it comes to alternative ways to solve staffing and wage cost issues.

I spend a lot of time talking to accounting firms about our story, and how we developed our particular offshoring model. After doing this for several years, I'm getting to a point where I've almost forgotten more than I know. That's a reflection of the ever-evolving business we are in. So I wrote this book to set out what I have learned in a nice, clear format for other firms to pick up and follow if they choose to. I will lay everything on the table, including the things that work and the things that don't work – and that includes some major screw-ups along the way.

I will share our story with you in the first chapter. The small accounting firm we started has spawned into a second business that regularly turns over seven figure sums in sales and employs over 200 staff (at the time of writing). It's been quite a journey and given the number of firms I speak to across Australia and the UK, and the number of staff I employ, I am well-qualified to speak on the topic of offshoring. We know why firms are struggling and we have the pill to cure the pain.

## Who This Book is For

This book is for accountants. If you run a different type of business, you can still use the information here, but you will need to consider the intended audience. However, most of the principles I teach will be easily transferrable to any business.

And to make things even clearer – this book is only intended for *forward-thinking* accountants. If you are not this way inclined, this book is just not going to make much sense to you.

You have probably either dabbled in some form of outsourcing or will at least be aware of its existence. A lot of firms I speak to have tried and failed at using an outsourcing model. I will discuss the key problems with that model later in the book. This is based on feedback from numerous firms who have tried it.

And most importantly, you must be a student. Come to the table with an open mind and a willingness to admit that what you've done before may not have been optimal. Then learn from other firms who are doing it better than you. I consider myself a lifelong student. I'm learning all the time, and I encourage you to do the same.

Accountants are experts and are always expected to have the answers - but I give you permission right now not to worry about having any answers. Read this book as a student and you will have the tools to change your firm for the better.

# Who This Book is Not For

If your firm is stuck in 1975, with archaic processes and approaches to work, along with stereotypical stuffy and dull personalities, I can't help you. Nobody can.

If you struggle to embrace change, this book will be the stuff of fantasy. You will not be able to connect our reality with 'your way of doing things'. You will probably write to me and tell me I have no idea what I'm talking about.

My communication style is direct. I don't sugarcoat my words, and I will tell you how it is. While it can be a bit in your face, most firms appreciate the raw honesty I bring to the conversation.

If you are a sensitive wallflower who will cringe when I tell you something is bullshit, best to put this book down now, go grab a cup of green tea and relax with a crossword puzzle.

If you need convincing an offshore model is the way of the future, this book isn't for you either.

I'm not an offshoring evangelist. I couldn't care less if you use an offshore team or not. All I'm going to do is share with you what we did with our own firm and what works and what doesn't work, based on our real world experience. I don't pretend to have all the answers...but I do have a lot of miles behind the wheel of my own firm and through guiding dozens of other firms to success with an offshore model.

## Keep an open mind

By the time you are done reading this book, you will have all the information you need to make an informed step forward as you research further into the offshoring or outsourcing model that best fits your firm.

If you keep an open mind as you read this book then I expect you'll find it helpful no matter what you choose to do with your firm in the future.

I believe your firm will struggle to compete, and even survive, in the future if you don't offshore work to a low cost country. And this is even more the case if you don't use current technology to produce your work. Hence the title of this book - '*Offshore or Die!*'

We all face death at some point, but in this case your accounting firm needn't die prematurely. It can kick on for many years through the turbulence our industry is experiencing at the moment and will continue to experience into the future.

*Buckle up - let's go!*

CHAPTER ONE

# OUR STORY

I'm sharing our story because it's relevant for you and most firms I speak to are intrigued by our business growth. As an outsider, I'm sure the story is interesting. As the dude with the steering wheel of this business in his hands, I find it part terrifying, part stressful, part exhausting and part rewarding. You'll find elements of our story woven into nearly every chapter of this book as I share with you what I've learned along the way.

That said, this chapter is just a broad-brush view of the last five years. I will give you a snapshot here before diving into the meat of our model in the following chapters. Don't skip this section, it's important for context.

We kicked off our firm in 2011, but we did it *differently.*

Most partners in accounting firms rise up through the ranks from graduate accountant, senior accountant, manager then partner, or some similar path to that.

I had a background in public practice as an auditor, but I ventured out and spent one year working as a financial controller in a Nasdaq-listed Australian subsidiary.

My intention was to become a business coach, and I felt working on the other side of the ledger in a company instead of just working as an outside auditor would be beneficial before I set out on my own. One of my biggest drivers is helping people, as solving problems energises me. And given my interest in and knowledge of business, coaching seemed like a good next step.

As part of my job as a financial controller, I was sent all over the world – an experience that opened my mind to the possibilities that existed beyond the Australian shores.

**Two key things happened at this stage:**

1. Xero accounting software was starting to take off in Australia.
2. I became acutely aware of the lower salary costs in the Philippines compared to Australia.

Thus, I conceived a model for an accounting firm in my mind – one built for the future. My plan to become a business coach was put on the shelf as a new idea took hold.

I would build a firm with my clients on Xero, and my accounting team would operate out of the Philippines. We would have minimal or no staff in Australia. If we did have any, their main role would be client-facing work and I'd want them to be highly experienced.

I'm often asked why the Philippines for an offshore team instead of India. The decision wasn't that complex. The cost is lower, I like South East Asia, their English is better and I don't much care for Indian food. Bottom line – neither is necessarily better than the other, it's just a preference.

My first visit to the Philippines in 2011 to check out the scene was an eye-opener. The heat was intense and suffocating, the traffic was insane and there was a heavily armed security guard on every corner. *"Where the hell have I landed?"* I often thought to myself during that four-day reconnaissance mission.

But, as with most things, you get used to it fairly quickly – well, no, that's not completely true, the traffic in the Philippines is something I will never get used to! I recently tried driving there and it's a nightmare. You have to watch out for people, dogs and chickens randomly crossing the road, other cars cutting you off, jeepneys and tricycles (Google them if you want a visual) pulling out in front of you with no warning, and many other obstacles. A taxi driver once told me, *"If you hit someone when you are driving, make sure you back over them. You have to make sure they are dead because there's less chance of the family extorting money from you than if you leave them alive."* Nice. Needless to say, I use Uber most of the time.

During that visit, I checked out several Business Process Outsourcing (BPO) providers. A BPO is a business where the staff members are provided along with workstations, computers and all the usual office requirements. Staff login each day and do work for their overseas employers. The Philippines is one of the fastest growing parts of the world for this type of operation. All the BPO clients had to worry about was training employees and managing their workflow. The BPO took care of the myriad of background tasks - legal, HR, payroll, internet, office, etc.

I was blown away with the work being done in these places and the modern office environments staff worked in. There is no difference between a modern Manila office and an office in my hometown of Melbourne, Australia.

I returned to Australia and informed my business partner, Jon, *"We're going to the Philippines!"* He was somewhat taken aback, but was solid in his support for my unconventional ideas and approach to business.

We engaged a BPO and commenced our recruitment process. I'll unpack the details concerning how this process worked later in the book, but for now all you need to know is that it wasn't easy for us.

Hiring staff offshore involved a lot more than just getting a warm body on a seat. Integration into your firm's systems and processes is critical to making an offshore team work. This is something most businesses get wrong when setting one up.

The first person we hired was Cherry, an accountant with a CPA qualification and a year's experience. She was the most enthusiastic candidate by far, and even read up on Australian capital gains tax issues to demonstrate her desire to work for us. To this day, having done more than 1,000 interviews, if a candidate arms themselves with some research and can demonstrate a desire to work with us, they almost always get hired. Most candidates don't bother, though.

Cherry's start with us from a work perspective was great. We couldn't have been happier. She was willing, able and did everything with a great attitude. Things were going well until she accidentally 'donated' all my stuff to a thief.

It was my second month in Manila and I had just landed from a long overnight flight. Being the kind, caring boss I am, I headed straight to the office to have an early lunch with Cherry without checking into my accommodation first. My normal routine was to leave a couple of credit cards at my hotel, in case I lost my wallet while out and about. I was very careful about this, except for this one time when I had all my stuff stolen.

**In my bag I had the following items:**

- Passport
- Wallet containing credit cards, ATM debit cards, identification and about P40,000 (US$900) cash.
- Car keys for my car parked in Melbourne.
- Glasses (I get a headache trying to read without them).
- An almost-new mobile phone along with my contact list.

I gave the bag to Cherry and said, *"Please watch this while I grab a drink."*

Cherry proceeded to break the number one rule when eating in the Philippines – don't put your bag under the table!

After lunch we gathered up our belongings to leave. The horrified look on her face told me that my bag was gone. The CCTV had recorded the fat bastard sitting behind us leaving with my bag some 30-minutes earlier. He was long gone.

So there I was, in a foreign country with no passport, identification, money, nor access to it. As you can imagine, I was very pissed off. But I had a new (and upset) employee watching how I would handle this speed hump, so I acted cool, calm and collected.

*"It's okay, Cherry, I didn't need all that stuff,"* I soothed. *"I can manage fine without it. Nothing to worry about."*

Inside, I was having a different conversation, *"What the hell were you thinking, Cherry? Or not thinking, to be more accurate. This is great. I have no money, no access to money, no ID and I can't see much without my glasses either."*

I told her it was all covered by my insurance and not to worry.

The next two weeks were spent in and out of the police station (beginner's mistake, police in Asia really don't care about foreigners), in and out of the Australian Embassy, and staring at my computer through a hazy fog while I tried to concentrate on work.

It wasn't until a couple of years later that I confessed to Cherry how my insurance only covered some of my stolen items. It became a long-running joke in our firm, and all new staff get to hear the story of Cherry giving my stuff away.

To top it off, I got conjunctivitis near the end of my two-week trip. I almost wasn't able to fly home. I wore a hat and looked at the ground to avoid eye contact with anyone. But at check-in they saw it and asked, *"Why is your eye pink?"* Of course, I replied, *"It's nothing, I just scratched it."*

*"Ok, no problem,"* the check-in lady replied and ushered me through. I looked directly at the ground every step of the way until I made it on that plane. No way was I not going back to Australia after a trip like that!

I still had to get through Hong Kong airport to connect with my Melbourne flight. As I walked through the terminal building, a guard stopped me. *"Busted,"* I thought to myself. But all he said was, *"Please remove your hat in the airport, sir."* So I complied and kept walking while looking at the ground. To build our business I was making this journey between Melbourne and Manila almost every month!

As time passed, we became more settled in Manila and having an office in the Philippines was just the way we did business. It raised a lot of eyebrows at first. I had people telling me to go to India instead. I had people questioning the logic of hiring a team offshore if you then have to train them. And I even had some people ask me if I was taking jobs out of Australia.

But the more time passed, the less people saw it as weird. In fact, a couple of years into our own journey other firms approached us to help them set up teams in the Philippines too. That was the last thing I wanted to do. So I referred them to other BPOs.

In mid 2013, we set up another office in Manila where we had about 14 empty seats. Space for our small team was hard to come by and we considered the excess capacity good for future growth. But, until those seats were needed for our own firm, we decided to offer a BPO service for other accountants.

We figured it might be a challenge to fill all 14 seats, but it would provide a small income stream to help pay some bills. It was never supposed to be a business in its own right. We only saw it as pocket money and to help out a few peers who wanted to duplicate what we had done in our own firm.

*Boy, were we wrong.*

**It went nuts.**

Over the 2014 calendar year, almost 20 firms came on board as clients of our BPO service and we hired about 70 people. We shared with the other firms how we ran our model, did training, what systems we used and how we managed the team remotely. As I write this in September 2016, we now serve over **50 firms and over 200 staff.**

We had learned so much through the school of hard knocks and we took it for granted that our experience would be of value to other firms. Jon and I found ourselves in the position where they were calling on us for help with all sorts of different issues.

In 2015, we realised that firms in the UK would probably have the same capacity problems as the Australian ones. So I got on a plane to London and spoke to many UK firms. In fact, I've now been to the country about 10 times in the last two years. It's been interesting watching this market develop. When I first arrived, firms were reluctant to change. They had been burned by Indian outsourcing companies and didn't have much interest in Xero.

But towards the end of 2015, and throughout 2016, they began to feel more comfortable with cloud-based tools, their awareness of our offshore model increased (probably because I gave away hundreds of copies of the first edition of this book) and the firms who trusted me and employed a team in the Philippines were getting outstanding results.

So the story continues to develop, but it's been quite a journey.

**We also picked up a few accolades along the way:**

✓   Winner: Most Innovative Accounting Firm, 2013

✓   Finalist: Most Innovative Accounting Firm, 2014

✓   Finalist: Best Place to Work, 2014

✓   Finalist: Best in Community Service, 2014

It will be interesting how the story unfolds. Watch out for the 3rd edition of this book in the future!

Maybe by then, I will have finally launched my business coaching practice…

CHAPTER TWO

# THE FUTURE OF THE ACCOUNTING PROFESSION

Let's talk a little about the state of the accounting profession, and where it might be heading. Yes, it's just a hypothesis, but there is a reasonable amount of evidence to support most of my comments. In fact, while talking about it for the last five years I've watched first hand some of these things actually taking place.

## Commoditisation of Compliance Services

Most business owners have their local accountant prepare year-end financial statements and tax returns. While there is some value in this, it's quite limited. The service basically keeps the business owner out of jail.

With the onset over recent years of cloud-based accounting systems and other technology, this process has become easier and easier for the accounting firm.

Cloud software companies are developing their products to catch the data (i.e. purchase) at the point it is created, enabling it to flow directly through the accounting software, correctly allocated, without it being touched by anyone. This means the business owner, bookkeeper and (heaven forbid) the accountant could potentially be bypassed on things that used to be bread and butter services.

Accountants often hear about value pricing certain things *upward,* but in the case of compliance services and bookkeeping, the price should be value priced **downward.**

Some forward-thinking firms will take a 'Ryanair' or 'Jetstar' approach, whereby they embrace the commoditisation and work out how to roll it out with lower prices on a large scale. Other firms will maintain their margins by including additional services that weren't on offer before.

Downward price pressure creates a threat to a compliance-based accounting firm. Your margins are going to be squeezed with lower prices and higher costs (salaries).

## Foreign Competition

Gone are the days when your biggest competitor was the firm up the road. Now you can expect to have firms from all over the world competing for your clients. How many times have you received spam from an Indian outsourcing company offering cheap accounting services? I get these emails several times a week.

But it's not just Indian firms anymore. There are accounting outsourcers set up in Vietnam and the Philippines. While it's still in its infancy, the rate of growth is staggering. It's easy to be dismissive and brush off this issue by assuming offshore equals low quality, and that clients automatically equate 'local' with 'good value', but you need to consider how your clients will react to an accounting firm who can produce not only the basic compliance work, but value-added services for half the price you are charging them.

What will be *your strategy* to respond to this threat?

## Cloud Technology

Cloud technology is making everyone's lives easier in the accounting world. The days of data entry are gone and the sending of files and receipts back and forth in a shoebox seems almost ancient. Yet many firms still accept this workflow approach, which is dictated by their clients.

However, the ability to *turn work around quickly* is also at our fingertips.

How long does it take you to prepare a bank reconciliation using traditional desktop accounting software vs a cloud-based product with automatic bank feeds and data rules for posting? This ease of use is making it possible for people anywhere in the world to do the accounting work for your clients. I have personally reconciled bank accounts sitting in airports waiting for my plane.

There are also products available so receipts and invoices are scanned by a third party and made available to your accounting staff for coding and filing electronically.

Data processing has changed. Have *you* changed with it?

# The Top Five Opportunities Facing Accounting Firms:

## 1.  Increase your gross margin

The largest expense for any accounting firm is **labour.** The salaries for accountants are very high and rising every year. I don't need to drop a bunch of statistics in here – if you own an accounting firm you already know this by looking at your P&L.

Some firms are now choosing to source their labour differently. Rather than having junior level accountants at home in Australia or the UK, they're employing staff in the Philippines to perform entry-level tasks.

If you take some of the costs and replace them with the same skills in the Philippines, the difference will go straight to your bottom line.

## 2. Increase capacity

We've observed the increased knowledge and competence of Filipino teams. It's more than just having an extra few 'sets of hands' to deal with low-level tasks (although this isn't a bad way to start). As their skills grow, so does the capacity of the firm they work for.

Firms that develop their teams well can continue to grow them *quickly and cheaply*.

As already mentioned, cloud technology will remove many non-essential tasks and give the forward-thinking firms an ability to take on more clients and add more services without necessarily having to add to their teams.

## 3. Increase your talent pool

There has been a shortage of accountants for a number of years, particularly in regional areas. For those firms starved of talent, the Philippines offer a large pool of experienced accountants to choose from.

The prevailing attitude of Filipino workers (in general) is of *gratitude* for their employment. This is more so than in Western countries, where entitlement and complacency can often be an unfortunate feature in the workplace.

## 4. Decreased turnaround time for work

Some firms (not you, right?) sit on clients' work for months. Their clients then get frustrated with the lack of response, accountants drown in the backlog and generally all parties are disappointed with the process.

On the other hand, there are firms who have an offshore team and are able to respond within **hours** (not days) to client queries, and they turn work around in **days** (not weeks and months). The client is happy, the accountant is happy and the owner of the firm is happy.

## 5.  Value-added work!

Clients don't just want their tax return filled in each year. That's the bare minimum service your firm should be involved with.

With all the extra capacity, partners and onshore accountants can get out and visit their clients more. They can find out what their clients really need from their accountant and design innovative services that make a difference.

Forward-thinking firms will leverage their distilled years of business wisdom into events and programmes for their clients that will help transform their businesses and lives. They will be able to walk alongside their clients and provide great advice *when the client needs it.*

The future of the accounting profession is *far from certain.* It is hard to predict what it will look like in five years' time. But one thing is certain - what worked yesterday, and even today, is fast becoming obsolete.

By focusing on how *you can utilise technology and offshore labour,* your firm can be well-placed to respond to, and take advantage of, the opportunities that are here now, and the opportunities that are going to present themselves in the near future.

CHAPTER THREE

# OUTSOURCING VS OFFSHORING

Definitions can be boring and they are often best left to expensive lawyers to work through. But it's important you understand a couple of important definitions. I see a difference between '*outsourcing*' and '*offshoring*', let me explain why.

**Outsourcing** a task means you are handing a discrete process or task to an *outsourcing company or professional* to *perform for you*. They do the work with their staff and return it to you. You can outsource tasks either in your own or another country and often pay by the hour or project. The point is, someone else is doing it for you using *their* systems. This means the work is being done *their way*.

Two common tasks here are outsourcing payroll to a specialist company to handle for you. Another one is using a company in India to produce your tax returns.

The way I see **offshoring** is that your work is being done offshore (obviously) by someone on *your own team*: an employee or contractor who *works for you*. They just happen to be in another location. And they do things *your way*, using *your systems*. I liken it to having someone work at home for you, only instead of them working just up the road, they are working in another country.

I don't see one model as superior to another. They are just different. And ultimately, it comes down to your preference. A bit like Apple vs Samsung. *Who cares?* Choose the one you prefer to use.

There are many ways to send work offshore and I'm going to discuss the five main ones. There are subsets within those methods, but we will focus on the major ones.

I'll work through each model, describing how they work and our experience with each one. *(We have personally used all the models, apart from the outsource model.)*

## The Five Main Ways to Send Work Offshore

### 1. Freelancer Websites

These are popping up all over the place. Back when we started, the two main choices were Elance or oDesk.

We used oDesk heavily in the beginning. It was great as a start-up business to get a website built for US$200 or telemarketing done for US$5/hr.

Since the first year or so, we've only used it intermittently for odd jobs.

We have spent more than US$10,000 through oDesk and hired about 150 contractors.

There are lots of great contractors on these websites. Unfortunately, it's tough to find them. Anytime I post an ad, I get inundated with dozens of unqualified and unsuitable candidates who rarely bother to read the ad in the first place. It's spam city and it reaches beyond oDesk itself. If you identify your company as the advertiser, potential candidates will hunt you down on Facebook, LinkedIn and Skype and take guesses at your email address so they can email you directly.

**Here's how I learned to eliminate most candidates *quickly*.**

→ At the bottom of my ad I say, *"Please write Accountants Rock! at the top of your application so I know you read this ad and can follow a simple instruction."* Most applicants don't do that because they either didn't read the ad or can't follow instructions.

→ You can see each candidate in a *preview screen* and by putting that simple instruction on the ad you can then delete them without having to open and read their application.

→ The next thing I do is *filter by hourly rate.* I know how much a fair hourly rate is in the Philippines, so when I see contractors asking for many multiples of this I delete them. And believe it or not, I do it in the other direction too. If someone is asking for US$1/hr or some other crazily low figure, I get rid. You're almost guaranteed a crappy outcome.

→ I disregard high feedback ratings. After hiring some terrible contractors with good ratings, I learned that most people give 5/5. Instead, *I look for a pattern of low ratings.* One bad rating isn't a deal-breaker because sometimes the employer could be a moron, but if it's a pattern then it's probably the contractor. Hit delete and move on.

→ In the end I'm usually left with **five to 10 contractors** who meet my requirements. Depending on the role, Skype interviews are booked and a decision is made. If it's a simple task, such as cleaning up a document, I simply send it straight over.

→ For other jobs, such as design work, I usually hire **three contractors**. I ask to see their work part way through and if it's sub-standard (I've seen some absolute shockers!) I end their contract and keep working with the one who *'gets it'.*

→ You'll also find that no matter how clearly you write your instructions for a job, most people simply *won't or can't follow them.* If you say, *"Do A, B and C",* they will come back having done A and C. You ask for B to be done, so they come back with an updated version of A and C, but this time they also did D. You didn't ask for D, but you will get it anyway.

→ Another thing to watch out for are contractors who **waste time while charging it to your job.** I've seen it all; contractors who are applying for other jobs while the clock is running on my job, spending time on Facebook or other unrelated internet surfing, and even watching porn!

Hopefully, the ideas listed above will serve you well should you choose to use one of these sites.

On the upside, I have had some *fantastic* contractors work for me over the years and it has saved us thousands of dollars. I've met some of them in real life, and even formed close friendships. But finding those sharp operators is trial and error. It's more art than science and now I cringe every time I feel the need to use one of these sites. I will only do so if it's the last resort. Mostly my Manila team deal with the oDesk contractors on my behalf, so I don't get involved.

There are many more positives and negatives about this type of approach to getting work done offshore, but hopefully I've covered just enough information to give you an idea.

In my opinion, there *are* better solutions out there. Yes, you will pay more, but you should save a lot of time. For small, 30-minute odd jobs, a freelance website like oDesk will be your best bet. If you're looking to place full-time staff and build a team, this type of freelancer website is the last place you want to be looking.

## 2. Independent Contractors

You can hire people full or part-time as independent contractors in the Philippines. There are several ways to do this. You can build *your own networks* so you can find staff yourself, or you can *use a service provider who will match you with contractors.*

Independent contractors typically work from home like the oDesk contractors. You will be responsible for paying them directly, either through a direct bank deposit, PayPal or some other payment tool.

The good thing about hiring staff in this manner is they are dedicated to working on *your* job. I have employed staff like this and found it to work very well. I set up a working area for my team in Manila and they worked together using my equipment. However, mostly you'll find that your team will be working from home under this model and providing their own computer and internet connection.

From a financial perspective, this model can be both good and bad for employees. We used to simply pay their gross salary into their bank account and then it was up to them to declare their own tax and organise their affairs when it came to government rules for contractors.

It's good for the worker because they get the full gross, but technically they are meant to declare and pay tax on this income. In reality, very few of them bother and I know the Bureau of Internal Revenue doesn't view the contractor situation in a positive way. That said, as an overseas 'employer', this issue is not really your concern.

If your team grows, managing it will become a challenge. Imagine having five contractors all working in different locations around the Philippines, communication will be much more difficult and you'll have to manage workflow, training and, of course, motivation. Essentially, they will be physically working alone.

All these things can be overcome with clever uses of technology, but I don't feel this model is ideal for accounting firms. It will be cheaper than other options, but it's a false economy. You will pay for it in other ways, most likely because of the inefficiencies associated with having staff in several locations: lack of monitoring and inherent unreliability in trusting someone to work alone in another country. A couple of locations are fine if you are keen, but the complexity will increase as you add more contractors. It's not impossible to manage, but it's much harder and more time-consuming than it needs to be.

## 3. Outsource Companies

This is the only model I have not personally used extensively. We did dabble in it and found the multiple layers of management in the outsourcing company painful and cumbersome to navigate. However, we understand the model well, and many of our clients have used it extensively. We investigated this model prior to coming to the Philippines, and for us the costs weren't as favourable as alternative solutions that existed in the market.

It's a great model if you are having **short-term workflow issues,** such as t*oo much work and not enough staff.* It can also be good if you have an immediate need to get work turned around. But remember, turnaround times can be out of your control.

The outsource model is famous in India and is quite mature in that market. You basically use the service on an hourly, part-time or even full-time basis, with different price points depending on the amount of time you use.

The upside of this model is there is a *lower training requirement* for your offshore staff. Due to the maturity of the market in India, many staff will already be familiar with foreign accounting and tax issues. This is not the case in the Philippines, where we are in the process of pioneering the market with an offshoring model.

Over the last couple of years I have spoken to numerous firms in Australia and the UK who have **failed with an outsourcing model.**

**There are two consistent reasons I repeatedly hear after a failure:**

1. Slow turnaround times
2. Inconsistent quality

With few exceptions, you *don't really have control* over the staff in these outsourcing companies. You pass the job to them and then you simply have to sit and wait until it comes back to you. The firms I've spoken to tell me this can take six to eight weeks in many cases.

Because you have so little control over staff, the outsourcing company can rotate employees through your job. The person who worked on your file last week may not be the person who works on your file this week, and the result is inconsistent quality. What's the point of outsourcing in this manner if you have to mop up numerous errors in the work when it comes back to you or explain the job multiple times?

If you are having workflow issues and can't get on top of things, my suggestion would be to **find a quality provider in this space and get some guarantees around those two high-risk areas concerning turnaround time and quality.** If you get those things right this model can work well for many firms.

## 4. Staff Leasing

Staff leasing is where a company in the Philippines (usually called a BPO) *employs team members on your behalf.* As a foreigner, you can't hire staff **directly without the correct corporate structure in place.**

The BPO legally employs the person but you are responsible for workflow and training. It's *your* employee. They are working directly *for you*, but simply sitting in a different location. With modern technology, this is almost the same as having the person sitting next to you. Not quite, but very close.

This is the model we specialise in, and we believe it's a great model for accounting firms that have a long-term view to create a low-cost, sustainable offshore team.

How it works is that you pay a fee per seat to the BPO, along with any salary and miscellaneous employee costs. That fee covers rent, internet, HR, legal, payroll, general management of the facility and some profit for the BPO.

**Your job is to train the staff and to manage their workflow.** The rest is up to the BPO. We pioneered this model for accounting firms in Australia and the UK after succeeding with it in our own firm. It's a great model because it enables companies to focus on what really matters (people and workflow) and ignore all the distractions (as the BPO handles these for them).

## 5. Incorporation

This enables you to **bypass the services of a BPO** when hiring a team offshore. Rather than using one to employ the staff and provide support and infrastructure, some firms choose to set up their own foreign entity and *do it themselves.*

*This is madness.*

How do I know? **Because I did it.** If I knew then what I know now, I probably wouldn't have done it.

**Often the accounting firm thinks they are going to save some money or improve their control over staff. It's a false economy, and ends up becoming a distraction for the accounting firm.**

Rather than guide you through a step-by-step procedure on how to incorporate in the Philippines, I'll just share my experience with you. If you still decide you want to go down this path, there are lots of legal firms who will be happy to take your money and help you set up your own company in the Philippines.

Before I incorporated myself, our staff worked as independent contractors. I had my team in a condo, and we were happily working away each day providing accounting and tax services to our Australian business clients. This was until I found out it was illegal to run a business from a condo.

*Oops.*

We engaged a law firm to incorporate us and my life has never been the same since.

In Australia, we can set up a company in about eight minutes. In the Philippines, **it took us about eight months**. And it was eight months of stress and *wasted time and money.*

From lawyers with questionable competence, to dodgy government officials, our journey never had a dull moment. By the time you are done reading this section, I expect to have persuaded you to think very carefully about this avenue.

**To complete an incorporation in the Philippines, there are three main government departments you have to deal with.**

1. SEC (Securities and Exchange Commission)
2. BIR (Bureau of Internal Revenue)
3. Mayor's Office

Let's start with our **capital structure**. When you start a company in Australia and intend to grow via retained earnings, you tend to capitalise it with about A$100 or so. To open a bank account in the Philippines I needed to capitalise it with P50,000 (around US$1,100). So we did.

We also had to have five directors and incorporators, **three of whom had to be Filipino.** So we structured ourselves. Jon (my business partner) and I had 24,999 shares each, and we gave one share each to three Filipinos we trusted. This meant we met the minimum legal requirements and didn't give control outside our existing business relationship, where Jon and I do everything 50:50.

The mayor's office is the department that issues the *'business permit'* allowing you to operate legally. Before issuing this permit they send an inspector or two to your office to ensure you are indeed running a legitimate business.

Two of these special characters turned up in my office one day with a big, thick file.

First, one of them started to interrogate me about my capital structure being 99.99% foreign-owned. Was this done quietly and privately? No way. Seems this was his moment to shine and he took the opportunity to perform in front of my staff.

*"My capital structure is legal,"* I insisted.

*"It's 99.99% foreign owned,"* he retorted.

*"The SEC has approved our company and capital structure,"* I argued.

We went back and forth a few times but seemed to get nowhere. I suspect logic wasn't his strong point.

Then it got even more interesting.

*"Your capital is P50,001 and your rent is P38,000. You will run out of money in month number two."*

Now, I'm a fairly open person, but to announce this in front of my staff seemed to cross some boundaries.

*"No,"* I said calmly, showing unusual restraint. *"We do intercompany invoicing and send money up to the Philippines every month. It's how most companies around the world operate if they have entities in multiple countries."*

*"No! You will run out of money in month two."*

Seems my logic was again falling on deaf ears. After going back and forth on this issue a few more times - in front of my team - I decided there was no point arguing and gave up.

I called my lawyer and she took over the conversation. Guess what the end result was? They issued me with a business permit where our apparent level of capitalisation was 50 times higher than it actually was. I still have that permit to this day, and it's unlikely to ever be changed to the real number.

This is just one example of what you have to go through to get your company set up in the Philippines. If your main game is accounting, this ends up being an expensive distraction.

Fast-forward many months and the **next major issue was ongoing compliance.**

The Australian government (who are a bunch of clowns in their own right) are nothing compared to the various government departments a business owner has to navigate in the Philippines.

Let me illustrate with some examples.

**Real. Life. Examples.**

You want to do banking? In Australia, we move money around electronically, but in the Philippines money has to be *physically* moved between two different types of banks. You either write a cheque or withdraw slabs of cash and stick them down your pants as you walk to the next branch to make a deposit.

I've done this.

*Lots of times.*

Remember when you were a kid and you held passbooks for your bank accounts? Well, it's still standard practice in the Philippines. Get off the plane and it's like stepping 30 years back in time.

Before you start thinking to yourself, *"Gee, this guy is a bit harsh,"* let me clarify. I love the Philippines. I love the people. One day, I will end up retiring there - if they don't kick me out first.

But trying to run a business is *nothing but a nightmare.* And dealing with any service provider, whether they are landlords, internet companies, banks or government departments, only compounds it.

Let me illustrate.

I wanted to obtain a visa that would enable me to stay in the Philippines as long as I chose to. This would mean I could come and go as I wanted with no time restrictions. It's called a Special Visa for Employment Generation.

The criteria? **You must employ 10 Filipinos**. My application was rejected despite the fact I employed around *80 Filipinos at the time.*

Why?

Because apparently, with my capital structure, it would be impossible to employ that many people.

Impossible?

Wow. A five-minute check with any of the several government departments we lodge employee payments for would have resolved that question mark.

Another government department in the Philippines is concerned with the Social Security System (SSS). Employers make payments there on behalf of employees each month and one of my team would stand in line, sometimes for hours, to hand over the paperwork.

One day, a member of my staff came to me and declared, *"Mark! Mark! SSS has gone paperless!"*

They had to pick me up off the floor as I keeled over in disbelief.

*"Bullshit. I don't believe you,"* I replied.

If they were going to be paperless it would save a heap of time each month. *"Yes, Mark! It's paperless. We simply have to put the documents on this USB stick and take it to them."*

*"We still wait in line, right? But now it's with a USB stick loaded with documents?"*

*"That's right, Mark."*

That's progress! And it gets better. SSS put a virus on our USB key that ended up infecting two of our computers.

You can't make this stuff up.

I just shake my head, mutter something to myself about incompetence and try to have a happy day.

If you go ahead and incorporate, this is what you will face on a *regular basis.* And remember, I have a great team around me and I live in the Philippines most of the time. To do this properly from another country would be a ridiculous undertaking.

So, those are the *five valid models* for either offshoring or outsourcing your work. It's up to you to choose the model that best fits your firm. There are no right and wrong answers, just preferences.

CHAPTER FOUR

# ETHICS OF EMPLOYING OFFSHORE STAFF

There are a few arguments that pop up from time to time concerning whether using offshore staff is 'right' or not.

I have to say, it's usually not the accountants who raise these issues. My guess is most accountants are focused on numbers and don't get too affected by social arguments.

## The Three Main Issues Regarding Employing 'Offshore Staff' Are:

1. Sweatshops
2. Slave wages
3. "Oh my God, all our jobs are going offshore!"

All a bit dramatic. But there is some truth in all of these issues. Not much, but some. Let me explain in a bit more detail.

### 1. Sweatshops

Yes, I'm sure they exist, I just haven't seen one myself, despite visiting numerous businesses in the Philippines.

So let's just say that while they are probably out there, they are few and far between. In the Philippines anyway.

Filipino workers are backed by a strong, employee-biased Labor

Code, which is enforced by the Department of Labor. The bias against employers is similar to that faced by employers in Australia.

Many people I speak to assume there are few rules and regulations. This is due to their perception of the country's global economic standing. They could not be more wrong. As an employer, I have to comply with a suffocating set of rules and regulations. These rules are there to protect employees from ending up in a sweatshop or being taken advantage of by a bad boss. However, the compliance burden on good employers is significant.

**Let me describe a typical office and working environment for a foreign company in the Philippines.**

- ✓ Staff work in modern, air conditioned offices that are equipped with the same technology you would find in the office of a western accounting firm. In our area in Manila, there are hundreds of restaurants, coffee shops, office and residential buildings, along with all the public transport people need to get to and from work each day.

- ✓ When staff work overtime, they get paid for it. Now I was never paid overtime as an accountant in Australia. I sometimes got time in lieu, but that is not the typical scenario.

- ✓ Employees get 20 days leave each year, along with a significant number of public holidays. Many workers also receive a health card for themselves and a dependent. Their employer usually pays for this. The health card is the equivalent of private health insurance.

- ✓ I can tell you that in our office staff work on new computers with dual monitors and up-to-date software. Hardly a sweatshop environment, is it?

The media love a dramatic story. They sell more newspapers like that, but the reality for most employees is that this isn't the case.

## 2. Slave wages

This is another popular topic for the media. Yes, there are places paying illegally low wages, but it's not the norm.

And yes, our staff earn a fraction of what their western counterparts do, but if you run the income argument, then you must run the expense argument alongside it.

I know most people in Australia spend what they earn, usually by buying useless crap. Most people end up with no savings at the end of the month.

The Filipinos are no different when it comes to saving, it's just the numbers are smaller and the spending is usually to support elderly parents or siblings going through college.

Remember, you need to look at both income AND expenses.

**Let's break down some numbers. You are an accountant so this will probably get you excited.**

→ Typical salaries for accounting staff are between US$500 and US$1000 per month. You will get staff outside that band, but most of them are within it.

→ A taxi in Australia costs about 20 times more than a taxi in the Philippines. A one-hour journey in my hometown of Melbourne costs in the vicinity of A$100, often more. A one-hour journey in Manila costs about A$5. And lately I've been using Uber, which is even cheaper.

→ A pack of cigarettes in Melbourne costs about A$20. It's less than A$2 in Manila.

→ How about a movie? At least A$20 in Australia. About A$5 in Manila.

→ The same ratios exist across other things such as food, accommodation and public transport. Cars and electronic goods aren't cheaper, but almost everything else is.

So, if someone earns the minimum wage in the Philippines, they will struggle. It's the same in any country.

All of our staff earn more than the minimum wage, and most earn much more. We recently benchmarked the salaries in our own business with a typical Filipino company. We realised we pay our staff at least 50% more than local firms.

So I can tell you firsthand that the slave wage issue simply isn't a reality for most employees.

### 3. "Oh my God, all our jobs are going offshore!"

*Hold on…hold on…not so fast.*

Yes, some jobs have gone offshore, and more will follow. But if you are in a role where technical expertise is required, such as dealing with complex company tax issues or significant client-facing roles, your job is safe. That will not be done offshore anytime soon.

There are a couple of ways of looking at this issue. Firstly, routine roles such as call centres or back office processing work are now predominantly done in places like the Philippines and India.

If I call any Aussie bank, my call will be answered in these countries. Tens of thousands of these roles have left Australia in recent years and they are unlikely to ever return.

I don't see the same thing happening to the same degree to accountants. The firm of the future, in my mind, will have client-facing staff in their home country, with the processing work (bookkeeping, low end tax work, financial statements, compliance, etc.) being done offshore in a cheaper location. Technology will play a big part, but I have my doubts as to the extent it will come into play anytime soon.

I can also tell you that although we employ a significant number of people in the Philippines, not one single job has been lost in Australia because of this. While more processing work is being performed offshore, Australian staff are doing more value-added and client-facing sales work.

And the reality is, most firms won't adopt an offshore model anyway. It's a place reserved only for the movers and shakers in the industry.

So yes, some jobs will move, but it's not as dramatic as the media makes out.

Therefore, as the owner of a firm, you ought to consider running it how you see fit, not how some nosey do-gooder (who has usually never run a business or employed anyone themselves) wants you to run things.

## How do Filipino Staff Feel About Working for Foreign Employers?

I get asked all the time how the Filipinos feel about working for Aussie and British businesses. So I asked a few staff to send me a note sharing how Frontline has improved their life, if at all. I think it's important that you hear from the staff directly, because they are the biggest part of what we do.

## Jenny

'Before Frontline, I was in the banking industry for more than seven years. For most fresh grads, it was a dream to work in a bank. I got a job in the biggest bank in the Philippines, which was owned by the richest family in the country. I always thought I was in a great place, it was very stable and I thought my career would turn out the way I'd dreamed.

I was at my very best - zero audits, accountant of the year awards and my staff level increased from year to year. Then I was transferred to a new manager and things didn't go so well. So I took a risk, went out of my comfort zone and gave up my seven-year tenure.

There was a big difference at Frontline. I was appreciated. That's when I gained more self-confidence and self-worth. I was treated like an asset that needed to be taken care of. Most importantly, the bosses here go the extra mile just to extend their help in all aspects of your life. They dedicate themselves to moulding people to be the best they can be. Because they're NOT GREEDY - which most bosses and business people are. There's definitely NO POLITICS - most Filipino companies have this. Here, if you're good, then you'll be praised and rewarded. If you mess up, you'll have to clean it up (but with the help of the people around you).

That's the difference between Frontline and all other BPOs, where staff just come and go. Here, people stay because they treat each other as family - and families stay together no matter what. And one thing I think our CEO doesn't realise is that he has provided a lot to many Filipino families. He's made their lives better and it will continue to be better, as he always puts us first. He's made an impact and provided inspiration to all of his Filipino staff.

With Frontline, I know I can build anything - a great career, a stable family, good relationships and a happy life.'

## Ciara

'My life now is different from how it was before. Working here at Frontline allowed me to experience life outside of work. I now have more time to do what I want after work and during weekends.

Before I felt that life was a routine. Wake up, then work, eat and sleep. Then do this again the next day. But now I've learned how to balance my life and work. Although I usually extend my stay in the office, I still have time to do what I want. This changed my perspective. Life is brighter and more meaningful. I am grateful that I am here at Frontline today. I never experienced this with my previous companies.'

## Dette

'Working at Frontline has made my life more productive, happy and meaningful. Since joining the firm, I've been able to accomplish more, both in my work and personal life.

My schedule has allowed me to have more time for my family, especially my daughter. My work also gives me the opportunity to learn new skills and undergo training.

I'm happy because Frontline has a positive working environment filled with kind and helpful people. My colleagues feel like family.

Finally, I have meaning because I am doing the job I love while making my clients happy.'

## Lei

'A year ago, Frontline took a risk and hired a fresh graduate with absolutely no experience. They believed in me and gave me a chance to be part of the HR team.

The great working environment and the constant encouragement and guidance from my bosses enabled me to hone my skills, learn new things and become more responsible.

Mark's advice and patience helped me grow and mature as a person. I became a role model for other employees.

Through the ups and the downs, Mark never fails to push me to become my best self. I love every moment of working for Frontline. It has a great team and even greater bosses.'

## Vivi

'Working with Frontline was a game changer for me. It really lives up to its principle of having a genuine 'work-life balance'. Work has now become interesting, rewarding and motivating. I always look forward to going to work every morning (even on Mondays!) because there are jobs to finish and I am pleased that my skills are being constantly enriched. My teammates are collaborative and there is a great team spirit in the office.

Most importantly, I have a clearer idea about customer service. I've also realised a great business is not just about providing fantastic service on time and building a good relationship with clients, it also concerns how it treats its employees.'

## AG

'I had this notion that when you get a job it should be in something that you already know. So if I'm used to working in the call centre industry, I should just stick with that. But I got tired of being in that scene.

Then a friend introduced me to Frontline. I was hesitant to try my luck as an administrative assistant because I didn't have any idea what that position even involved. But being a call centre agent wasn't challenging for me at all. I wanted to be where I can use my brain.

And here I am. I've been working at Frontline for almost two years now. If they can see my potential and believe in me, why can't I? I didn't imagine I'd be doing great with the tasks given to me and I'd never have imagined myself doing the things I do now. But I was wrong and I am doing it. As the days go by I'm getting better and better.'

## Anon

'I had a bad experience with my previous employer. He is old and a maniac that wants his employees to wear skimpy clothes at work. He wanted to make me his personal secretary and I refused. When our manager submitted the performance evaluation (with salary increase), I got the highest grade and was recommended for the highest increase amongst the employees, but my boss refused it and gave me only half of what was recommended.

When I joined Frontline, I got a boss who is not only nice but cares about his staff members' well-being. He is a bit strict but also fair. I have the best experience here.'

## Jo

*'Because of our work schedule here, I now get to enjoy time with my family. And knowing that my parents are not getting any younger, I am always grateful for the extra time that I get to spend with them. Before I had to leave the house to go to work before everyone woke up. I arrived home when everyone was asleep. This meant I sometimes felt like a stranger, especially to my nieces and nephews - I only got to talk to them once a week.'*

## Zendy

*'Frontline improved my life because I believe I've developed my social and communication skills. I've also learnt how to be strong enough to face everyday challenges, especially when it comes to gaining more knowledge. Here at Frontline Accounting, learning never stops.'*

## Anon

*'Since I started working at Frontline, I've learnt many things and explored new topics in accounting, especially for Australian clients.*

*I've learnt how to be more detailed in financial reports, which makes me more confident in what I am doing.*

*I feel happy when my boss is commending me and this increases my motivation to do the best in my field.*

*I feel like I am improving every time I finish jobs for the clients. This is because they are satisfied with the work I am doing, and it's all from Frontline.*

*I am very grateful to belong in this family.'*

## Minette

'For years, I have struggled looking for that perfect job where I can find the balance between work and family. Here in the Philippines, you always have to choose which comes first. So I often feel the guilt of spending more time at work and less time with my family. (Plus the commute, which takes hours!)

But when I stumbled upon this job opening at Frontline, I thought to myself, 'I must have done something good for this blessing!' We have the perfect working hours, plus days off and holidays. It's just perfect. Don't forget about the benefits! Man, they're really gracious!

The working environment is also very light and fun, but we still mean business. Those were the job traits I have always prayed for in order to spend more time with my family and support them to the best of my ability.

Frontline has been, and always will be, a blessing in my life and my family. I am truly grateful for the opportunity they gave me to work in this company. That's why I'm highly motivated to give them my best - this company deserves nothing but the BEST.'

## Ria

'Mark and Jon are the only employers I know who care so much for their staff. They always think about what's best for us. They also always motivate us to do better, not just in our work but also in our personal lives. I never thought that I would be working for a good paying company where I didn't need to do too much overtime and didn't get too stressed. I am so glad that I still have time for my family and friends.'

## Phen

*'To be quite honest, it's usually Filipino bosses rather than foreign ones who take advantage of their staff.*

*What I've experienced and seen here at Frontline is far from what I've gone through in the companies I've previously worked for.*

### A. Training and self-development

*At Frontline, we've been encouraged (pushed) to find ways to learn more, improve ourselves and grow. We have a small library here and it's free to borrow any of the books in it. If that's still too limiting, we're also given access to Mark and Jon's Kindle.*

*If there's any training we want to take (that's related to our job, of course), we're always made to feel we can approach them about it.*

*I've requested training in some of my previous companies and I've always ended up being turned down due to various reasons, reasons that Sir Mark would call BS...(Longer story: I've worked for a well-known multinational company that turned down my request for additional training due to budget restrictions. Get this, though, I knew someone from the training department and after I left she told me there's always a budget and they were just waiting for a request from our manager to start looking for possible training programmes for the staff. It seems our requests, which we'd been making through our Filipino managers, weren't even reaching other departments, let alone higher management.)*

### B. Dealing with achievements and mistakes

*At Frontline, we are not only held accountable for the mistakes we make, but we are also recognised for all our achievements.*

*I've been part of companies where the staff members take the fall and the managers take all the glory.*

*I've had bosses not leaders.*

## C. Open door policy

A lot of companies boast that they have this open door policy where you can approach management with anything.

Well, I've only really seen it carried out here at Frontline. Seriously.

Mark and Jon are pretty open with us and they expect us to be open with them as well. Before deciding on something that may affect us they make sure to either ask for our opinions on the matter or inform us about what will happen.

Can you imagine that? Our opinions matter! (Even though some of them can be deluded at times.)

Do you know how great that feels?

And this is not just for show.

Oh, and while I'm on the matter - have you ever seen an employee approach their manager (CEO for that matter) with a PERSONAL problem (usually in tears)? I've been one of them and it's something I've never done before or felt like doing.

This only happens when members of staff feel that their bosses really care for them.

If these things don't convey how far from being taken advantage of we are, I don't know what will.'

**Mark's note:** These staff comments were requested when I explained how some people in Australia and the UK think we take advantage of people in the Philippines. You can see here how Phen is quite passionate about arguing how well we take care of people!'

## Blanca

*'Before starting work at Frontline, I didn't know if I would be able to adapt to this kind of environment, where I am surrounded by lots of accountants!*

*It turned out to be a good thing, though, because I'm very willing to learn a lot of things and I do enjoy working as an admin assistant.*

*One big thing that's happened to me is that I've had the opportunity to go to Australia for training. It's been my dream since I was in high school to visit the land Down Under.*

*I am blessed with having Mark as our president at Frontline. I never expected anything, but I am always surprised with what he does to make his workers happy.*

*I'm thankful for my two bosses, as they are so generous and thoughtful. I'm also grateful for our teammates in Newcastle, as they were so patient with their training.'*

## Rose

*'Since I started working with Frontline, I have enjoyed being part of a family rather than just a regular company. Our bosses genuinely care for their employees and always want to know how we are doing personally and professionally. They make sure that we learn and grow professionally, without sacrificing our personal life, which includes family time. Our bosses also recognise and appreciate hard work and let us know that our ideas and opinions matter.'*

## Chrisalyn

'I didn't know how to put everything that has positively affected me down in only one paragraph, so I decided to make two standalone ones regarding the top two things I love about working here: work-life balance and less/no paperwork. I hope this helps.

**1. I came from a local company with an eight to six working shift pattern plus overtime, five days a week.** Most of the time I needed to work on a Saturday too, especially if it was audit season. My life revolved around work. But when I moved to Frontline everything changed. I now work a seven to three shift, five days a week, with no overtime. This means I have enough time for work and more time at home, which equates to a great work-life balance that we all strive to achieve.

**2. Being an accountant is a tough and stressful job.** I am grateful to have found Frontline, which provides a friendly environment to lessen the stress of our work. In a country where accounting relies mostly on paperwork, I am thankful to have a job in a paperless, cloud-based company.'

## Jennifer

'From my first interaction with Frontline, I realised the company was fully committed to offering the highest level of service to its clients.

As time went by, I discovered that they were also doing that for their staff.

This company allows me to maintain a great work-life balance. I thoroughly enjoy the culture and working environment, and the management always make themselves available for questions and new ideas.

*In the 12 years I have been working, I can say that this is the most rewarding and best time of my career.*

*As long as you have the determination to work hard, there are no limits to how far you can reach. If you want to work in a good environment, you can join any place, but if you want to work in a great environment, this is the place. Here, your team makes your job fun and interesting.'*

### Dianne

*'I value my time a lot and Frontline has given me exactly that.*

*With my previous company, I barely had time for dinner, myself, my family, or anything else I wanted to spend time on.*

*Working here means having more time for whatever the heck I want.*

*I also love that no thick lines are drawn between the management and the employees, meaning we treat one another like family.*

*Frontline is a growing company and I can feel that I'm growing with it.*

*I also know that Mark, Jon and the rest of the gang have my back if ever I go through a rough patch. It's nice to know that you never have to go through things alone, even if you want to.'*

### Bhella

*'I am a new employee and my life has changed in just a short period of time.*

*Firstly, this is because of the financial aspect of my job. I used to be content with what I received on payday, even though I received less than the work I did. Today, I receive equal or more. This is why I want to give my very best.*

*Secondly, the management is not hard to work with. They are approachable.*

*Finally, I enjoy a good employer-employee relationship. Frontline doesn't do business only for money and provides its employees with opportunities. The company treats us as part of the family. It is not common for a big company boss to sit beside an employee and ask how he/she is doing - yet they do.*

*I'm lucky to be part of this growing company.'*

So, the myths surrounding the ethics of using offshore staff are just that. *Myths.* When I explained to my staff how some people in my country think we take advantage of them, they actually laughed out loud. They couldn't reconcile in their minds how well they are treated with the misperceptions in western countries.

Employing staff in the Philippines is a good thing. Not only do you help the employee, but in many cases you also *raise the standard of living for their whole family.* But don't take my word for it. Jump on a plane, visit us and see for yourself.

CHAPTER FIVE

# HOW TO WORK WITH AN OFFSHORE TEAM
## By Jon Ryall

**Author's note:** *Jon is my business partner and as far as I'm concerned he's the brains behind our business. Jon is brilliant at training staff, developing systems and dealing with technical accounting issues. I've asked him to write this chapter, which describes the mechanics of running a firm with an offshore team. It's based on our real world experience. I encourage you to take the things Jon shares here and modify them for your own firm.*

\*\*\*\*\*

For most accounting firms, working with offshore teams can be a whole new and unfamiliar world. The team isn't physically in your office, so what's the best way to communicate with them? How do you know if they're working hard? They look busy, but are they effective? Are there cultural differences that make it harder to hold staff accountable for mistakes? What tools should you use? Ultimately, how do you ensure that you don't put a heap of time, energy and money into building up a team only for it to collapse and go to waste?

I've had many years working as an accountant in firms both large and small. I've also spent a number of years building my offshore accounting team and I have good news. The principles of building strong onshore teams also apply to your offshore team. If you have a firm with a great culture, this can be translated to your offshore team. The *method* is the same, but the *mode* has changed.

This chapter will outline principles that bring success to any business (the method). But it will also show you how to set things up and deliver them in a 'multi-office' environment (the mode).

Some firms will have many of the elements in place already. If so, setting up your offshore team will be quite easy. If this isn't your firm, work through the chapter slowly and develop a plan for each section.

I promise it will save you a huge amount of time, headache and money!

## The Team Performance Formula

A few years back, I was involved with a small networking group that included an insurance guy, a lawyer, a tech start-up owner, a non-profit CEO and me, the accountant. As we talked about building our businesses, the conversation moved to team culture. Paul Durham (the lawyer) spoke up and said, *"There's a formula for this. It goes Systems multiplied by Training multiplied by Monitoring = Culture."* Now, I find culture to be a fairly vague word, so let's change it to Team Performance.

**Systems x Training x Monitoring = Team Performance**

Let's stop there for a moment.

Think about the current state of your accounting firm or business. How would you score out of 10 for each of the three inputs? Write those numbers down on a piece of paper. Then *multiply* them to give you a score out of 1,000 (you could also then divide by 10 to put it into percentage terms).

| Systems | Training | Monitoring |
|---|---|---|
| ✓ You have a systems manual for the firm.<br><br>✓ Checklists for staff to follow.<br><br>✓ You use predominantly cloud software.<br><br>✓ There is a consistent work methodology.<br><br>✓ Technical resources are available to staff.<br><br>✓ Good IT infrastructure (internet, hardware, etc.).<br><br>✓ Workpaper templates exist.<br><br>✓ Clear job descriptions with an 'outcome' focus.<br><br>**Workflow systems**<br><br>✓ You have a 'Playbook' (set of dos and don'ts for the team).<br><br>✓ One-page business plan. | ✓ Training is regular and scheduled.<br><br>✓ There is a documented training plan, which is a mixture of technical and non-technical.<br><br>✓ You train your team to understand how your business works.<br><br>✓ Staff are encouraged and enabled to 'go beyond' with self-study.<br><br>✓ Delivery is interactive (not passive).<br><br>✓ You have a new employee ('boot-camp') curriculum.<br><br>✓ You have a way to build relationships, not just skills (i.e. team building).<br><br>✓ Team members have the opportunity to run training (teaching is the best way to learn).<br><br>✓ You encourage 'product champions'. | ✓ You create clear expectations at the start of jobs.<br><br>✓ Daily and weekly workflow meetings.<br><br>✓ You have ways to measure productivity.<br><br>✓ Awareness of cultural and personality differences.<br><br>✓ Regular performance feedback.<br><br>✓ Deadlines and milestones visible and accountable.<br><br>✓ Workflow systems visible to everyone.<br><br>✓ Firm does 'one to one' catch ups with staff.<br><br>✓ Annual or six month appraisals.<br><br>✓ Support for staff in need. |

The defining characteristic of the Team Performance Formula is that a zero score in any of the inputs results in complete failure of the output (a zero for Team Performance). In fact, all three inputs need to be strong to get a reasonable output.

They are like three pillars or the sides of a triangle.

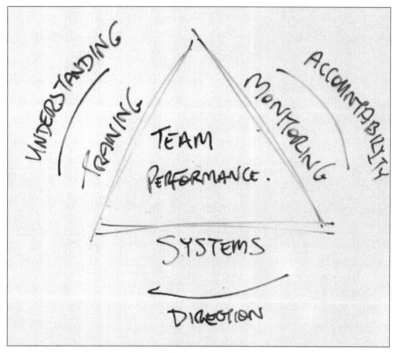

*Figure 1. Team Performance Formula*

I immediately knew this was the formula that applies to successfully running an offshore team.

When it relates to accounting firms, many of the issues we see in offshoring stem from a deficiency in one of the three factors. In some cases, we advise firms that offshoring is not a good solution until they sort some of these issues out.

Good systems provide *direction* for your team. If you have no systems in place and just run your practice off what's in your head, guess what? Your team will have no clue what process to follow, your training will be long and hard, and they will become dispirited when you hold them accountable for non-performance.

Systems are just the start. You then need to *train* your team to give them *understanding* of how to use the systems properly. Without training you might have an eager staff member who gets your checklist and goes into 'processing mode', but does it all wrong. All you get is a mess. You can imagine the disaster on your hands if you combine this with no follow-up and monitoring.

With good systems and training, you should start getting quality outcomes from your team. But unfortunately, most employees don't think like business owners and without *accountability* productivity suffers, staff get roadblocked and, at worst, you could end up with behavioural issues that make you wonder why you hired anyone to begin with!

The common theme for the remainder of this chapter is that **what's good for the offshore team is also good for your firm as a whole.** In fact, I'll avoid using the term 'offshore' and just refer to the 'team', which means both your offshore and onshore employees.

If remote work is a new concept for you, then your focus may need to shift from running a business in a single location to running it in multiple locations. While it's very common for businesses to run this way, it's not so common for smaller accounting firms. It can require a paradigm shift.

I will mention some of the common tools that many of us use with one caveat - the tools are changing at a rapid pace.

New, highly-funded software start-ups are launched all the time. Yesterday we used Skype, today we use Zoom. What will we use tomorrow? At the end of the day the emphasis shouldn't be about the tools, it's about the *outcome.*

But you can't ignore the tools either. Keep an eye out for the changes or ensure someone in your team is. A great way to do this is to be involved and collaborate with communities of like-minded practitioners (like other Frontline clients)!

## Systemising Your Practice

When we started Frontline Accounting, there were virtually no documented systems. I was a great accountant, but all my knowledge was in my head. We also had no prior year workpapers.

When we hired our first offshore CPA, Cherry, it was my job to train her, help her to develop and keep her productive.

It was **_hard_**.

I remember the first job I delegated to her. I emailed her the client files, then called her on Skype. I calmly and carefully explained the requirements of the job, how the software worked and what she needed to do on each workpaper. Section by section. It was accompanied by a lot of head nodding and *"yes sir"* on her part. (Had I paid more attention, I would have also noticed she was not taking notes!)

I left her with the job and called back around lunchtime for a progress report. I was secretly hoping to find a completed or almost completed set of accounts and tax return, but to my dismay almost nothing had been achieved. The referencing was wrong and she'd been locked out of the tax software and needed my help with that also.

So the next step was to *reverse delegate.* If you're unfamiliar with reverse delegation it means the staff member has meekly attempted but fallen short of job completion so they delegate upwards - to their boss - to complete it for them. There is nothing more frustrating for a partner of an accounting firm than reverse delegation.

I reluctantly opened TeamViewer (screen sharing software) and together we worked on her computer remotely. I performed all of the tasks for her, with her passively watching her screen.

For the next couple of months, a lot of training was done this way.

It was a good thing we didn't have Work in Progress reports in those days. I'm sure Mark would have been quite unhappy about the write offs!

Eventually, Cherry picked up the fundamentals like all young, bright accountants do, and over the next two years I trained up other accountants in this way.

The one advantage I had was that after Cherry became proficient, she was able to train Sam and they both then trained Jesseca, Ana and eventually Adhel.

But I wasn't having fun.

With the revenue we were making at the time, I sometimes wondered if it would have been easier if I downsized the team to zero and just did all the work myself.

The business had grown and was incredibly reliant on me. I was spending all my time Skyping from person to person, helping with roadblocks and trying to encourage productivity.

My team thought I was amazing - I was the answer to their every problem. On my birthday, one of the team Photoshopped Superman and put my head on it. They all said, *"Happy Birthday, SuperJon!"* We all laughed.

But I had a phone call a few weeks later with my business coach. We were brainstorming on what to do to improve our firm's results and he noticed how much I did for everyone. *"Your team probably think you're Superman!"* he said.

Yes, in fact they did! How did he know that?!

So the first project we did was to get all the knowledge out of my head and into a manual. Once done, staff were no longer allowed to ask for my help if they hadn't first checked the manual.

## Your systems manual

A firm with a systems manual is always more valuable than a firm without one.

Your firm will only Scale Up to the degree that it is supported by quality, easy-to-use systems.

In the context of an offshore accounting team, you will want your systems manual to be online (not a huge Word Doc or PDF) and read like the help page of a good website. It should be well structured and ideally have a combination of checklists and visual screen shots or short videos. If you're not tech savvy, don't worry, this can all be driven by your team using very cheap or free software.

I've included a snapshot of the front page of our Systems Manual. (See figure 2, on page 95)

There are many providers of checklists and processes for accounting firms. These can be handy, but in my experience they are often too long and detailed because they are trying to apply to *all* firms rather than *your* firm. Given your firm is probably a unique blend of software tools, services and methodology, you can make your own manual far more specific and useful to your team.

| Topics | **FRONTLINE ACCOUNTING SYSTEMS MANUAL** |
|---|---|
| + 1. WORKFLOW 4 | |
| + 2. SALES 3 | **1. WORKFLOW** |
| + 3. CORPORATE SECRETARIAL AND STATUTORY DOCUMENTS 4 | 1.1 Workflow Flowchart |
| | 1.2 Workflow Note |
| + 4. BOOKKEEPING 8 | 1.3 Menu of Services |
| + 5. MANAGEMENT REPORTING 3 | 1.4 CockUp Register |
| + 6. QUARTERLY BASs/IAS 2 | |
| + 7. FRINGE BENEFIT TAX 1 | **2. SALES** |
| | 2.1 Customer Relationship Management (CRM) |
| + 8. YEAR END 10 | 2.2 Creating Proposals |
| + 9. SMSF 2 | 2.3 On-boarding a Client |
| + 10. SMSF AUDIT 6 | |
| + 11. ADMIN 27 | **3. CORPORATE SECRETARIAL AND STATUTORY DOCUMENTS** |
| + 12. TRAINING 5 | 3.1 Setting up a Company, SMSF and Trust |
| + 13. CLIENT QUERIES 7 | 3.2 ASIC Annual Review |
| | 3.3 Updating Company Registers |
| + 14. Trello 0 | 3.4 Preparing Trust Distribution Minutes |
| **Other Resources** | **4. BOOKKEEPING** |
| Frontline Accounting | 4.1 Setting up an Organisation in Xero |
| FRONTLINE ACCOUNTING SYSTEMS MANUAL | 4.2 Creating Invoices in Xero |

*Figure 2. Snapshot of our Systems Manual*

If you're currently subscribed to one of these services and happy that it works well for you, then that's fine. You may choose to create additional procedures around admin tasks and very specific tasks, such as booking travel, that are unlikely to be in an off-the-shelf product.

Once built, it requires just minimal maintenance and updating. It is most useful for new staff who will heavily rely on it in their first few months.

It also becomes a form of accountability, as quality issues can usually be traced back to staff who deviate from the set procedures.

If you've never built your systems manual, don't be daunted as it can actually be done quite quickly, as long as you do it the right way.

As an accounting partner, you simply don't have time to build the process manual yourself. Our 'Version 1.0' took a single team member about 12 weeks to create on a part-time basis. That's probably more time than you want to commit along with everything else that normally needs to be done.

## Here is the six-step process for building your systems manual

### 1. Plan out the project

Allocate two to three hours and involve all team members who can contribute to building the manual. If you're a small firm like we were, that is everyone. If you're a larger firm, you might select a small number of people or break it down by division.

Get in front of a whiteboard (or mind map software if online) and write out the 'Divisions of Labour' within your firm. It could be sales and marketing, tax, wealth planning, audit, admin, and so on.

Under each of those, plan out what procedures need to be documented - we came up with 58 when we did the exercise. These can then be added to project management software or a spreadsheet to be managed by the Project Champion.

### 2. Choose your Project Champion

The criteria for this person are that they need to be good with detail and a good finisher. This person won't generate all the procedures for the manual, but will monitor progress, keep the spreadsheet or software up-to-date and upload the approved procedures for publishing.

### 3. Leverage your team

Against each process, allocate who will create each one. The project champion can then delegate, and they can get to work.

### 4. Capture, review, publish

This is the 'tools' step that tends to generate a lot of questions. It also has the potential to either bog down the project or help it to progress at rapid speed.

Your team are the ones with the time and focus to get this done quickly, but they will need management help from time to time, particularly when they don't really know the procedures you want.

**Here are some dos and don'ts for your involvement:**

*Management Involvement - The Dos*

- ✓ Create a Minimum Viable Procedure (MVP). This is nothing more than quick dot points that the team member can then fill out with screenshots and detail. (This concept came from the Sweet Process website).

- ✓ Use screen capture software like Jing or Snagit. Actually perform the basics of a procedure on screen while the software is recording. The video can then be instantly uploaded online and passed to the team member who will transcribe it into a stepped procedure.

- ✓ Link to already existing procedures, external websites (which often have great help pages). For example, I have a subscription that provides all kinds of checklists and templates - my Systems Manual simply tells the staff to access the site and download the appropriate checklist or letter template.

*The Don'ts*

- ✗ Expect perfection - there's always time later to tweak. Just focus on the MVP.

- ✗ Reinvent the wheel. If a procedure exists on someone else's website, just link or refer to it.

Once a procedure is finalised, it can be uploaded into your online manual (published). Tools you could use for this are shown below, in the 'useful tools for this section' table.

**5. Weekly check-in meeting**

Book in time to spend with your Project Champion to review progress, overcome roadblocks and approve final procedures. Accountability is vital for a large project like this.

**6. Systems maintenance**

Once completed, the systems manual needs to be maintained over time. My PA manages our manual and from time to time checks the external links and often adds procedures.

Whenever something outside the norm happens, or a major client error occurs, you should ask, *"What does the manual say?"* If no procedure exists, have the staff update for the benefit of future team members.

## Useful tools for this section

The following are *suggestions only*. Research is recommended for current best practices or new and better products.

| | |
|---|---|
| For hosting your systems manual | Screen Steps, Sweet Process, Google Sites, Confluence |
| For recording screen shots and short videos | Jing, Snagit |
| For project management | Asana, Trello |

Now that your Systems Manual exists, onboarding your offshore team and training them up has become so much easier and faster.

It's now time to focus on the *Workflow Systems.*

## Workflow Systems and Strategies

Running an accounting practice is inherently difficult. There are many steps, many moving parts and people with varying skill levels pushing work through the various stages in the factory.

Setting up our firm using cloud software, offshore labour, fixed pricing and bundled packages, I always had this feeling that the firm had different economics than a traditional accounting firm.

I have already mentioned that we had no Work in Progress for the first few years. Living without timesheets was bliss for the staff. Our write offs would have been bad, but at the same time we had very low labour costs and overheads. So how did my team know that they were doing well? Alternatively, how did they know if they needed to pick up their game? What was the number one Key Performance Indicator (KPI), and how did we (and still do) measure it?

### The number one KPI

My question was answered after reading *'The Goal'* by Eliyahu Goldratt. In this classic book, which is narrated in novel format, the factory became wildly profitable by recognising that 'productivity' is not the key. Rather, the factory can only produce a finished product at the rate of the *slowest step in production.*

In other words, the biggest bottleneck in the system will be the determining factor on how quickly goods are completed and sold.

Without going any further into the theory (I highly recommend you read *'The Goal'* by Eliyahu Goldratt, *'The Lean Turnaround'* by Art Byrne and pretty much anything else to do with Toyota and Lean

Production), I decided that the number one KPI for my firm was **Turnaround Time**.

If I eliminated every other KPI, but could consistently drive down turnaround time, more work would churn out the door and get billed and my capacity could grow as the team required more work to keep them busy. This would mean I could take on more and more projects, my Average Hourly Rates would increase and I'd be doing larger write ups, not write downs.

Further to this, the biggest hindrance to driving down turnaround time is **bottlenecks** in our workflow. As in the books already mentioned, bottlenecks are often hidden.

## Bottlenecks are the enemy

If you're running an offshore team, or running multi-offices, the complexity is increased. As a result, there is opportunity for more bottlenecks, particularly where inter-office communication is poor.

At this point, you'll probably be realising what I realised - I'm the *biggest bottleneck*. That big list of file reviews that is weeks old is hurting the factory.

Some accounting firm partners think that setting up their offshore team will solve their workflow problems. If they are the bottleneck, it will simply add to their daily list of team queries, help needed and unfinished work.

An offshore team is anything but a solution for workflow problems. But it will increase capacity where the bottlenecks have been removed.

**It's for this reason that I always encourage my offshore team members to:**

- ✓ Go directly to the client with their queries.
- ✓ Call clients on the phone - don't email and wait three days for a response.

✓ Do their research before coming to me with a query (I'm a bottleneck).

✓ Call the taxation office directly and find the solution.

✓ Call the software provider directly and get the solution to that bug or issue.

> Encourage the team to take initiative and do more. Don't limit them.

I've heard of other providers of offshore services recommending that accounting firm clients only allocate low level work to the offshore team. For example, they can reconcile accounts to trial balance stage, then pass the file to the onshore team who will do the financial statements and tax return.

If the offshore team can do the whole thing, why not let them? Less steps and handovers equal less bottlenecks and higher revenue.

Others hide their team from the clients so that a manager or partner is the only one communicating to their client base (even on low level queries). Again, that puts more work on the manager or partner and creates bottlenecks.

I'm not saying you should let your offshore team loose on your clients without supervision, but the goal is to make it fast and easy to complete a job and get it billed, preferably by the team and not the partner.

## Assessing your workflow system and practice tools

I could never recommend what workflow tools you should use. Firms just vary too much. Instead, I'll outline **four of the main hindrances** to your workflow and things to look for when assessing your overall workflow system.

## Hindrance #1: Not easy to access

Data security is important, but when working with offshore teams your data lockdown attempts can make things cumbersome and slow for your staff. There are ways to keep things secure, but make sure what you do doesn't mean staff are constantly needing IT support to fix things or speed things up.

## Hindrance #2: Not easy to collaborate

I'm a big fan of Google Apps for this reason. They make collaboration super easy. The amount of time saved by not having to always keep multiple versions of files is huge. To optimise offshore teams, you really do need either Google Apps or Office 365.

As an example, instead of sending a client letter back with amendments to be made, you could get the offshore team member onto a call and both be working in the live file. It is fixed in one go, the staff still gets the training that comes out of a review, and the job is done and out the door without the need to go back and forth multiple times.

## Hindrance# 3: Not easy to review and update

Ideally, you shouldn't be doing a lot of printing to get work done. Back in the mid 2000s, we were keeping largely paperless files at Deloitte and it's now possible to run an entire practice without paper. We've been doing this in Frontline since day one. There are workpaper platforms where you can prepare, review and finalise files and accounts, all online.

## Hindrance #4: Not easy to see

When we started Frontline in 2011, we immediately enrolled in Rob Nixon's coaching club. They advocated a best practice for workflow, which was the white-board system; you monitor what jobs are in progress, who is doing them and how long they have been in the office.

Every firm needs something like this, although it's more difficult where offshore teams are involved. For that reason, it probably needs to be an online tool, or a spreadsheet at bare minimum. One of the firms that have staff in our office actually runs two whiteboards concurrently - one in each office.

## The Tools

I've made a brief mention of some tools in this section and I'll continue to bring them up throughout the remainder of the chapter. At last count, I have more than 30 software subscriptions that I have bookmarked and use regularly.

At our quarterly mastermind meetings, we sometimes joke that we need a software subscription that can manage all our software subscriptions. I know some of us yearn for one that does it all. But I'm not sure that's going to happen.

I liken it to 'Grandad's tool shed' vs a 'Swiss Army knife'.

My grandad had an amazing tool shed containing all kinds of specialised woodwork apparatus. As much as one Swiss Army knife would have been easier to own and reach for than all those tools, he could make things in that shed that a Swiss Army knife never could.

Given our profession is very technical and complex, we need specialised tools for specialised purposes. The good news is that as technology adapts, the tools are linking up and communicating with each other more and more, making our lives easier.

Now that your team have good systems and tools in place, the direction is set for them. In the next section, I'll show you what we've learned about how to train your team to upskill them *fast*.

## Training your team

Awesome accounting firms *invest in their people*. They always have and they always will. Just as all good firms provide development opportunities and training to their staff, they also extend this to the offshore team.

Training is all about **transferring understanding** into your team. Understanding the needs of your clients, understanding what your practice stands for, understanding the technical knowledge required for the job and understanding what needs to happen to kick goals within their role.

But transferring understanding between people can be hard and slow, let alone transferring understanding to someone in another country and from a different culture. Typically, it requires an investment of both time and money.

One thing I've noticed from talking to other Frontline firms is that when their first accountant starts to deliver some really good results, they start to realise how much investment they might lose if the person leaves. I get that because it used to worry me too.

But by the end of this section you'll see how losing a key member of your offshore team can be more like a bump in the road rather than a major car wreck.

I've already explained how *not* to do it - that's the slow way. Let's now move the vehicle into the fast lane.

## Accountancy Training in the 21st Century

I think the education industry is in need of an overhaul. There's definitely pockets of disruption going on here and there, but for some reason most training providers just pile everyone into a single room and deliver boring information that is expected to be regurgitated on an exam without questioning if it could be done better.

Translate this to the accounting industry and it's even worse. Boring topic plus boring delivery means learning is an uphill battle all the way.

With our offshore business model, I knew I needed good training.

I had already done a lot of training myself but wanted to speed it up by also paying for some external coaching.

There were many options, but very few delivered the training *online* and of those that did, much of it was *overly technical*, which makes learning a lot slower.

## What most firms want from training

I liken training up your offshore team to training fresh accounting graduates. They start up with you having no experience in overseas tax systems (UK, US or Australia) and therefore have a steep learning curve ahead of them.

### Boot camp

The first training for any offshore accountant should be 'boot camp' style, focusing on technical skills and, to a lesser extent, software.

If you're 'going it alone' in your offshore adventure, this is going to be a big challenge for you. It definitely was for us. It will require a lot of time input from managers or partners, or potentially outsourcing to a training provider (who will usually make the training too technical).

Fortunately, we have now developed an eight-week interactive training programme for new Filipino accountants who will work with Australian clients. The UK programme is currently in development. The Aussie programme took us several years to develop and is constantly being updated and improved. It combines the required technical learning with actual work and supervision by experienced Filipino accountants. It can also be customised to the needs of the firm - depending on any specialisations they have planned for that new hire.

We also include some 'culture training', which educates the offshore staff on differences between western and eastern work practices, language and communication. We share some of the 'quirks' they might face talking to Aussies and Brits.

Whether you create this training yourself or get Frontline or someone else to do it, the investment will be high. But the payoff is real. This is one of the reasons I no longer fear losing a trained employee. I know I can get another one up to speed relatively quickly.

> Great accountants pick up the technical skills quickly, and while they won't be experts in eight weeks, they can become a productive team member after this time.

You generally only need to do this a few times. Once your offshore team is competent, they will become the new trainers as you grow your team, decreasing your time, input and cost substantially.

## The elements of effective training for your firm

**There are a number of methods to upskill your team both in technical and non-technical areas. Great training will ideally have the following elements:**

✓ Customised and interactive

Can be tailored to the needs of the user and put into their language. Often involves activities and interaction so that they get 'hands-on' learning.

✓ Leveraged

This is where the training can be used over and over again - usually because the session has been recorded for later use. You may sacrifice some customisation, but you'll save time and money in the long run. I'll spend more time discussing this later in the chapter.

✓ Delivers technical improvement

Mainly focused on local tax laws and local practices. It's more challenging to deliver this in a non-boring way.

✓ Delivers non-technical improvement

Delivers improvement in employee confidence, firm culture, English speaking, writing and 'soft skills' such as team building or self-development.

✓ Return on investment

Labelling something 'cheap vs expensive' is difficult as it depends on the outcome of the training. Most firms are willing to spend good money on training if it delivers a strong return.

## The options for training an offshore team

Below I've listed some of the training possibilities you can use for your offshore team - all of which I've tried personally (as have many other firms).

→ Tax boot camp

This is essential for a new offshore accountant. It can be customised and requires a larger upfront investment, but it accelerates the learning. It's like an 'on-ramp' to the highway, providing a 'speed up zone' to get the employee to the required motorway speeds.

→ Overseas trip: staff come to you

Many firms arrange for their staff to visit Australia or the UK and work in their office for a period of time. Again, this is an investment by the firm, but it delivers good technical growth and is a great experience for the team member. The new accountant gets the opportunity to build relationships with the onshore staff and observe how they work in the office. In some cases, the Filipino employee may never get another opportunity to travel to the comparatively expensive country. If managed well, this can therefore increase loyalty and engagement in the team member.

For additional technical growth, the firm may also send the employee to a local seminar or workshop. This isn't a leveraged form of training, but it does still benefit both the employee and firm.

→ Overseas trip: you go to staff

Nothing substitutes face-to-face learning and relationship building. As per the above, doing the occasional trip to the Philippines allows you to observe your team in their work environment. You can customise training to their needs and work through jobs on the desk next to them. After work, take them shopping or to a local restaurant, bowling alley or karaoke bar. You'll be surprised how well the 'non-work' activities can break down the walls between cultures, facilitating confidence and communication between offices.

Some firms even take this a step further by organising short 'team building' events or trips. The Philippines has some amazing islands and resorts, which are not overly expensive. One firm asked his staff to arrange a team-building day in Manila. They took the day off from work and spent it at a waterslide park!

→ Face-to-face online training

This can be structured or unstructured. Our current preferred tool to deliver this is Zoom software, but Skype, GoToMeeting, Lync or Hangouts are also fine. You can share your screen or PowerPoint slides or stand in front of a whiteboard (your team watch you onscreen).

To deliver this effectively (and not put people to sleep), get your staff to interact by solving problems, doing role play or even have them delivering the training to their peers. Make sure chocolate is involved to reward those who interact (get someone in your team to purchase and distribute it).

Once, after some continued frustrations about certain team members' lack of organisational skills, I decided to run training on 'How to Get Absolutely Organised' (GAO). I delivered a quick presentation on how I do it and set down a challenge for the team. They were to spend a week researching and then present to the group the following week on what their personal strategy for GAO would be. There was a small cash prize for the most creative presentation - decided by vote.

All of them returned armed with interesting and creative PowerPoint presentations, and I must admit I was super impressed!

→ Webinars and tax updates

Unfortunately, most technical training isn't delivered online. This makes it harder for training your offshore team. There are, however, a few around and if you go down this road look for the provider that brings technical aspects into common language. In Australia, my personal preference for online training is Knowledge Shop.

In my opinion, tax updates have limited use for both offshore and onshore staff. I remember sitting through, or rather enduring, monthly one-hour lunch sessions at a previous firm learning about the latest court cases, which rarely had anything to do with my existing clients.

Ongoing technical training is necessary for all accountants, but make it count. Try not to give staff training that is downright *boring or irrelevant to their role.*

→ Technical reading

Ideally staff members have access to this so they can look up specific issues. Like all accountants, they need access to resources. But again, it's fairly boring and ideally shouldn't be the only source of training.

→ Software certifications

At the time of writing, almost all of our accounting firm clients use Xero for their accounting software. We make a point of getting all staff (accountants and non-accountants) through the certification process.

There are many other training courses, mostly online, that relate to various cloud software products and can be useful. They also require no time input on the partners' part.

It can bring benefit to the firm by allowing individual staff members to develop expertise on particular software products that clients and other employees typically need help with.

→ English training

Some staff are great as a technical accountant, but their lack of people skills and communication can limit their career growth. Maybe you've worked with staff like this in your firm. I certainly have.

The Philippines is the same. Some staff are very shy and need to develop confidence speaking with westerners, both inside your firm and potentially to clients and suppliers.

For these staff members we prescribe a few things. Online email training for structuring and writing their emails and Toastmasters for learning to speak in front of groups and developing their English skills and confidence.

We host a Toastmasters group in our Manila office and some of the transformations in the team have been very noticeable.

**To summarise all of the above, look at the table on page 111.**

## Leveraging your training

Most of the training I've described above is somewhat structured. But every accounting file you review is an opportunity for training. Your team should be learning and growing as they do their work, and they should understand and clear the review points generated by you or your managers.

Unleveraged training is 'ad-hoc' and 'one-to-one'. In other words, you notice that the employee doesn't understand something so you bring them into your office or get them on a call and explain to them how to solve the issue.

This is one of the reasons it takes many years to develop staff. Being the 'trainer' is also one of the challenges for you, as it diverts time and energy away from other areas of growing your practice. Recording your training and building a knowledge bank is therefore critical.

| Training Type | Customised /Interactive | Leveraged | Technical Growth | Non-Technical Growth | Assessment |
|---|---|---|---|---|---|
| Boot Camp | ✓ | ✓ | ✓ | ✗ | **Essential** |
| O/S Trip: Team to You | ✓ | ✗ | ✓ | ✓ | Build Skills, Relationship & Experience Firm |
| O/S Trip: You to Team | ✓ | ✗ | ✓ | ✓ | Build Skills & Relationships |
| Face to Face Online | ✓ | ✗ | ✓ | ✓ | Customise, deliver, record, repeat. |
| Webinars and Tax Updates | ✗ | ✓ | ✓ | ✗ | **Boring but Essential** |
| Technical Reading | ✗ | ✓ | ✓ | ✗ | **Boring but Essential** |
| Software Certific-ation | ✗ | ✓ | ✗ | ✓ | Useful and low touch |
| English Training | ✗ | ✗ | ✗ | ✓ | Optional |

In Australia, one of the more difficult reconciliations to do is a GST reconciliation (this would be VAT in the UK). Junior staff members really struggle with this, and I recall constantly training staff and fixing their errors. That was until I recorded a 20-minute video on how to reconcile GST. This was uploaded to a private YouTube channel and made available to all future staff and trainees in boot camp training.

At the time of writing, that particular video has been viewed 82 times. I've effectively provided more than 27 hours of employee training and it took me 20 minutes to make. No one asks me how to do GST reconciliations anymore, and they arrive in the file correct for sign off almost every time.

What current processes in your firm drive you crazy? With the right tools you can record the video, make it available to all staff and even link it into your systems manual.

Once you've built up a collection of training resources, you can arrange and organise them in a basic staff intranet site.

## Help your team to help themselves

As I mentioned earlier, I needed to transition away from being the 'source of all knowledge' for my team. Part of doing this involved making sure they had access to good resources for technical queries.

If you are a partner, you'll no doubt have plenty of these resources already. Make sure your team have access and know how to use them (perhaps this could become a training video).

*Internally, I created a rule when staff were roadblocked with a technical issue. It went something like this...*

**When you have a technical query you will:**

1. Search for the answer on Google, then if needed...
2. Search for the answer in (insert your technical resources website), then if needed...

3. Ask a peer, then if needed...
4. Ask Jon, by which time you should be able to present him with some suggested solutions.

It didn't initially stop the team asking me questions, but I would respond with the question – 'What did Google say?'

**The message got through quickly enough.**

## Team self-development

I think one of the best things you can do for your team is to teach them the value of **taking ownership** of their own learning and career. Here are some things we have done internally to foster this:

### Book reading competition

Every employee of Frontline Accounting is required to read at least one book per month from the team library or elsewhere (they can choose any nonfiction book that will help them grow). The employee who reads the most books for the year receives a prize. These are summarised on a spreadsheet and each person shares what they are learning at the monthly team meeting.

For this to work, partners need to lead by example. Seeing as you're reading this book, this clearly goes without saying for you. For the first six months of 2016, our team had read about 200 books between them.

### Further studies

We tell our team that we will subsidise training that relates to and brings benefit to their work.

My PA chose to undertake a course on 'Accounting for Non Accountants' so she could understand our industry better.

## Useful tools for this section

The following are *suggestions only*. Research is recommended for current best practices or new and better products.

| | |
|---|---|
| **For hosting your training videos** | YouTube, Vimeo, Screencast |
| **For recording short, on-screen videos (5 minutes or less)** | Jing, Snagit |
| **For recording longer videos and webinars** | Camtasia (PC), ScreenFlow (Mac) |
| **For online communicating with staff** | Zoom, Skype, GoToMeeting, Lync, Hangouts |
| **Training Site/Intranet** | Google Sites, Sharepoint, Confluence |

# Putting it All Together: Your Training Plan

There are more than enough ideas shared in this chapter to super-charge the training of your offshore team. Many firms do these things already. If you're feeling overwhelmed with where to start, take an hour or two and decide what works best for you.

> Try and use a combination of training approaches and develop a plan.

In particular, you could develop a *'training pathway'* for a new team member. What should they learn in the first three, six and 12 months?

**Make a checklist of required training** - then put it in your system's manual.

What sort of resources could you include in a staff training site? Can your team build it for you? Again, make a list and an action plan to get it done.

Remember, what's good for the offshore team is also good for the onshore team. You may realise that you've been neglecting the training of your employees in general. Perhaps you can leverage your time and do training for your entire firm.

Employees in your office, your country and those around the world want to learn and grow. If you help them do this they'll become more loyal and motivated and you'll be well on the way to *superb Team Performance in your firm.*

## Monitoring performance

Not every employee experience in the Philippines ends with a success story.

Just as in your own office, employees have financial issues, marriage issues, health issues, mother-in-law issues, boyfriend issues, pet issues - you name it. And then there are the downright bad employees. I'd like to think we filter them out pretty well, but occasionally one slips through the net.

One such employee was my first PA. This is a different PA to Mark's first one, whom he describes in Chapter Nine. We both failed in our first PA hiring attempt. My PA was trained in an international call centre, had a great phone voice, was super friendly and charmed everyone. Whenever I Skyped him he'd be smiling on screen. I heard lots of *"yes sir"* and *"I'm on it now!"*

I thought I was onto a winner. At times I wondered why his projects were taking a long time to complete, but I was super busy and just put it out of my mind. Then I heard a rumour he'd been caught sleeping at his desk (during work time). Someone else commented how he often walked aimlessly around the office.

My view of 'Golden Boy' had suddenly shifted. All of a sudden, I became suspicious about why my projects were dragging on. It eventually came to a head when he decided to make Valentine's Day office decorations instead of finalising some urgent tasks. Mark ended his employment the same day.

> My lesson was: I should have been more aware of what he was doing with his day.

There was a lack of *accountability*, which meant that with all the great intentions I had for this guy, his performance went under the radar and he was able to bluff his way through.

Working in a multi-office environment and monitoring performance has some added challenges.

You can't necessarily see the non-verbal cues that indicate someone isn't engaged with their work. These include slouching in their chair, daydreaming and taking extended toilet breaks.

How do you make sure there is peer pressure in place to ensure employees 'work while they're at work'? Seven hours of work is what you pay for and seven hours of work is what you should get.

For the remainder of the chapter, we'll look at the strategies used when offshoring to improve visibility of the team's results, offer support when they need help and ultimately impose *accountability* for Team Performance.

## Making the invisible visible

If you've already attended to the '*systems*' section of this chapter, a lot of this should be done already. Good systems and workflow tools will make the results **visible.**

If you aren't getting the results you need, the question becomes why? Have you identified and attended to the bottlenecks? Are the team clear about what they need to do and how to do it?

## Visible workflow

By making people's work visible to everyone, there is an inherent accountability. Everything must be visible. You need visibility over regular workflow, small tasks, large projects and communications.

## Accounting work

One of the reasons why Rob Nixon and the Panalitix group recommend a whiteboard system for your accountants is because everyone in the office can see it. They can view the jobs listed, see who is doing them and how long they are taking.

I love working with whiteboards, but it's not as practical when you have different people in different locations. So you need an online tool to manage workflow.

I personally like Trello software. It is like an online whiteboard with cards you can move around and group together depending on the workflow stage. You can map out the columns according to your workflow: Ready to Start > In Progress > Under Review > Completed. Each card is one job and can move to the next stage of production once ready. Due dates are visible, as are assigned employees.

It was designed with *Lean Production* in mind, and there are ways to make bottlenecks in your workflow stand out. And it's free! I'm hearing that more and more accountants are starting to use Trello for workflow.

Our Trello board (See figure 3 on the next page) gets referred to every single day in our huddle. We attach workpapers to the cards and converse about the job in question. Each card keeps a full history of the job, so I keep a copy of it on our server once completed.

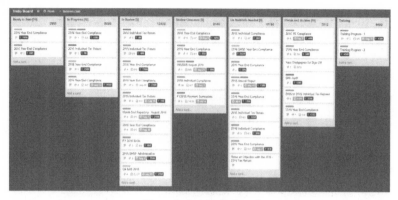

*Figure 3. Our Trello board*

You don't have to use Trello. As you read this, there may be some new breakthrough product that's even better. But think through the elements listed here and how they might be useful for improving visibility on the jobs you delegate.

As an accounting firm, you may be running work in progress, monitoring timesheets, turnaround times and billings. Don't hide these from your offshore teams. As long as the expectations are reasonable, they will respond to your KPIs just the same as your local team.

## Administrative work

Administrative assistants tend to take on a combination of routine work and can also be involved in projects such as organising an event or publishing your systems manual.

For routine work, the main requirement is that nothing gets missed. I'm often forwarding emails with various small tasks and I used to find that once the request left my inbox, it left my mind.

Having email tools to remind me about small tasks to follow-up is essential.

I also use Trello for smaller projects (one card per project) and regularly check in with my PA to discuss progress.

For larger projects, a whole new Trello board (online whiteboard) might be necessary, or you could look at a 'list based' programme like Asana.

## Useful tools for this section

The following are *suggestions only*. Research is recommended for current best practices or new and better products.

| Workflow | Trello |
|---|---|
| Projects | Trello, Asana, Basecamp |
| For email follow-up and reminders | Hiver, Resnooze.com, FollowUp.cc |

## Accountability for your offshore team

Now that workflows and projects are visible, you can implement more strategies for holding your team **accountable** for their results. Like your onshore team, your offshore lot need to know that you're *watching* and that *results matter*. They also need to know you care about them.

If you're the sort of boss that likes to *rant, criticise publicly or respond in generally emotional ways*, proceed with caution. All people, in all cultures, have a general need to be treated with respect.

In the book *'Crucial Conversations'*, the first step in approaching a difficult employee conversation is ensuring they feel *safe*.

When trust is established, you can hold people accountable and build a team that engages *towards the goal together*.

→ Creating accountability with a daily huddle

A lot has been said about 'daily huddles', 'stand-up meetings', '10:10 meetings' or whatever name you choose to call them. The main thing here is that you catch up with your team daily to discuss work and identify roadblocks.

In his book '*Scaling Up*', author Verne Harnish outlines how daily huddles are an essential part of any growing business. Adding employees grows complexity *exponentially* and without a team meeting each day, your finger is no longer on the pulse.

We've tried various approaches to our daily huddle. For a time, we felt they were boring and useless so we stopped doing them. It didn't take long for the problems and 'surprises' to surface in the business, so we quickly implemented them again.

I don't think there's a 'magic pill' for a daily huddle. If it's not working, change up the routine. How we run ours today may not be how we run it tomorrow.

**The main elements to a good huddle are:**

1. **Daily targets**. For us, this is billing and production. I make sure the team know where we stand in relation to the Team Performance for the month.
2. **What are you working on?** What have you accomplished today? The focus should be on *done*. As in, when will your job be done? (Getting staff to commit to deadlines in front of others is brilliant!)
3. **What are your roadblocks?**
4. **What have you got planned for tomorrow?**

If your huddle is run well, the whole team will know if the results aren't great and everyone needs to push harder. You'll also have a feel for when jobs are going off track. If someone is badly underperforming, you'll notice this too.

→ One-on-ones

Your role as leader in a business is also one of **coach**. This extends to your offshore team also. Ensure that either you or someone in your firm is spending enough *one-on-one time with them*, helping them identify areas for improvement. This could involve the occasional informal webcam chat or visiting the overseas office and taking them out for coffee to chat about work. You'll find one-on-ones super valuable.

If you have problems with an employee, you should provide feedback *quickly and directly*. Often, your team member will open up about personal problems they have in their life and this is your opportunity to provide practical support, or make allowances with their work.

> Don't implement one-on-ones in response to bad performance. Do it because you have a desire to coach and grow your team.

→ Regular feedback

When working with your offshore team, keep in mind they don't always see the client responses to their work. If a client is unhappy about something, make sure the staff member is aware of it. How you deliver this is important, but don't hide it and then get frustrated when the problem recurs. Likewise, share publicly when one of your offshore team over delivers.

Create **clear expectations** for your offshore team members. Show them what will make them succeed in their role and how to get promoted. If they are underperforming, tell them directly what the expectations are and what they did that violated them.

In all of this, make sure you are **listening**. Most staff want to do a good job. There are times when instructions have been misread (maybe you should have spoken on Skype rather than emailing), or technology has got in the way. Perhaps one of your systems isn't working as well as it could and needs changing.

Be direct, but also be *open-minded.*

→  Formal appraisals

There is nothing new about formal appraisals in the accounting profession, and they should also extend to your offshore team. Make sure you include them in the appraisal process and reward them for good performance.

Also make sure that nothing is a 'surprise' when it comes to formal appraisals. If a team member is underperforming they shouldn't find out about it this way.

## Providing support

There have been many times when Team Performance problems weren't the team's fault. Our offshoring business has grown at a rapid rate over the last few years and this has put them under tremendous strain.

As your team is held accountable, you'll find problems could be a skill issue (generally fixed by more training) or an engagement issue (a decision to fix on their part). As discussed in other parts of this book, some people in the Philippines face issues that you and I won't ever have to.

Be the sort of person who wants to help and support your offshore team, both professionally and personally. Have boundaries as you do this. After all, the business is the reason you are both working together, so the business should be the priority.

**Support could take the form of:**

- ✓  Additional training
- ✓  The offer to get counselling
- ✓  Financial assistance (in extreme circumstances, and for limited amounts)

✓   Time off work

→   Speaking up

Employees also need to speak up. Encourage your offshore team to do this. Their natural inclination is to assume that you know what is going on in their jobs, but they need to understand you don't.

Having a daily huddle will go some way to spotting roadblocks they are having, but don't accept silence day after day when you raise the issue. If they have no roadblocks, they probably aren't being stretched enough. Every business has them and the team need to let you know what they are.

## Final comments about working with your offshore team

Hopefully, by now you've realised that working with your offshore team is actually quite straightforward. Many firms already have the elements in place, and the offshore team will just require a few extra tools to become a natural extension of their firm.

If you have a lot to work on, or this chapter is overwhelming, just remember that what's good for the offshore team is also good for the onshore team. By implementing these things into your practice, you will find yourself with more free time, better productivity and more profit.

# CHAPTER SIX

# RECRUITMENT

I've personally interviewed *more* than 1,000 job applicants over the last five years. I couldn't tell you the exact number. On some weeks I interviewed 20 people. By the end of a week like that, I didn't even know my own name, let alone have the ability to recall any details about the candidates I met.

Most of the staff who get past the interview stage succeed in their role. I've received no formal training in interview technique; my recruitment process has been developed through trial and error from the ground up, and I couldn't tell you the first thing about accepted recruitment theories. But I'll take real world experience over the classroom any day.

My company has received more than 15,000 job applications in just the last two years. And we now have a team of eight people across recruitment and human resources doing what I used to do on my own. My style is unconventional and difficult to duplicate...just ask anyone on my team! Fortunately for you, I rely on a series of obvious red flags during recruitment, which I will share with you in this chapter. Unfortunately for you, I also rely a lot on gut feeling. As you work through this chapter, don't try and copy my style - just be yourself and adopt the principles I teach you. Do enough interviews and the gut feelings will come anyway. If you are good with people, you'll be a step ahead of those who aren't. And if you use a BPO, they will do the heavy lifting for you.

## Hiring Our First Employee

Not only was this our first Filipino employee, but it was the first time I'd employed anyone. *Ever.* One of my friends was a human resources specialist at a large Australian bank. I remember going for a walk with her and her husband one evening in the summer of 2012 and talking about how to recruit someone because I had no idea what to do. That's how green I was. It's funny now when we catch up and I tell them we have employed more than 200 people!

We used a generalist BPO during our first six months in the Philippines. A generalist BPO is one that recruits for a wide range of roles in a team and/or a wide range of business types. For example, they might have a bookkeeper, a marketing person, a graphic designer and some call centre staff. In contrast, we are considered a specialist provider. Across all our staff, about 60% are accountants, 30% are administrative support and the other 10% is marketing, IT and other miscellaneous roles. So we do fill other roles, but we don't make a habit of building a team full of wide-ranging job descriptions. They are usually just supplementary roles for an existing team of accountants. About 90% of our clients are accounting firms. We know this market better than anyone and we are what you would call a specialist BPO.

While this section might come across as a bit harsh on the BPO we first used as a client, I can assure you we had a good relationship with them. But there were lessons to learn, so I'm going to share them with you as I walk you through the process we experienced. Then I will take you through what we do in our BPO as a specialist. You will see the difference between a generalist BPO and a specialist. Back when we started, specialists didn't exist for accounting firms. We were the first specialist to launch a Philippines-based BPO for accounting firms in Australia and, to the best of my knowledge, in the UK too.

Once we engaged the BPO, we provided them with a job description for our prospective employee. It formed the basis of the advertisement. We were looking for someone with three to five years' experience in Australian accounting. They needed to be able to handle GST, personal, trust and company taxation, financial statement preparation, bookkeeping and various other tasks you'd expect of a senior level accountant.

We then sat back and waited for applications to roll in.

And we waited.

And we waited...

Nobody with matching skills applied. In fact, nobody with skills even slightly resembling what we were looking for applied. It's because nobody like that existed. If they did, it was a tiny proportion of Filipino accountants. I didn't know it at the time, but we were going to pioneer this model for other firms one day. And by the way, out of the 15,000+ people who've applied for jobs with us over the last couple of years, only a handful have been exposed to Australian accounting. And the exposure was generally quite low level. We've never had anyone walk in who can do Australian tax.

So that's your first lesson if you use a BPO to recruit staff for you. The BPO we used had no idea of the type of applicant we wanted, they just took our requirements and started hunting without *really understanding* what we needed.

We realised that if we wanted to hire someone we'd have to adjust our expectations fairly quickly. So, we accepted candidates from corporate backgrounds instead of public practice accounting. And we accepted we would need to teach them Australian accounting. The BPO also didn't understand their own salary levels. They quoted us a salary range in the beginning then tried to get us to adjust upwards as we went along, in order to fill the role with a good candidate. It was frustrating - we went by their guidance and believed it. But their guidance wasn't much more than a guess.

We reviewed a bunch of CVs and chose the candidates we wanted to interview. I can't remember how many exactly, but it was around six. We set appointments with them all to do Skype interviews. This was because Jon and I were in Melbourne and the candidates were in Manila. These were the first interviews I'd ever done - Jon had some experience interviewing when he was at Deloitte.

For me, the interview process was torture. And it was probably even worse for the candidates. Firstly, nobody at the other end introduced us to each candidate, or helped facilitate the interview. We just opened Skype and the candidate was sitting there.

Normally in a social situation, there would be some small talk about the weather or something else to break the ice. Not in this case. The candidates were so terrified they only gave us one-word answers. We lost count of the times we heard, *"Yes, sir"* and *"No, sir."* I enjoy a good conversation, so I was ready to stab myself in the eyes with a pen trying to get these candidates to talk. I ended up giving up on most of them. Jon is much more patient than me, so I simply stopped talking and asked him to drive the interviews. For me, it was important to get to know the applicants. The plan was for me to visit Manila each month and train one person, but I refused to travel that far and sit next to a person who refused to speak. Fortunately, out of the half a dozen applicants, one had a personality.

To this day, I still remember her cheeky answer to the question, *"Where do you see yourself in five years' time?"*

*"I'll either BE a financial controller, or I'll MARRY one!"* she told us enthusiastically.

Finally! We found someone with a sense of humour. Jon and I got on a plane and spent a few days in Manila to do a final round of interviews. Cherry's final interview was a continuation of her initial - very politically incorrect - one. I hate rules, so I like someone who is comfortable being themselves, even if their jokes are cringeworthy.

*"Tell us what you know about Frontline,"* we instructed her during our face-to-face interview.

She looked at Jon and said, *"You were an auditor."* She then looked over at me and with a cheeky smile said, *"And YOU were a financial controller!"*

It was part uncomfortable and part hilarious. So we hired her. And five years later, she still works for us. Her vision for her future didn't quite pan out, though. She's been a very successful senior accountant for us, not a financial controller. And she got married and had a baby, so she now works at home for us part-time. Her husband isn't a financial controller, either...maybe her new son, Marcus, will be!

## Generalist vs specialist

I'm now going to share with you our approach to recruitment. I'm not trying to suggest we have *all* the answers, as nothing in recruitment can be perfected due to the fact there are people involved. And no matter what you do, it's just not possible to predict how some people will behave. But our process does work. We only hire about one per cent of the people who apply for jobs with us, and most staff succeed in their role.

What I want you to do with this section is study the **principles** I share, and contrast the way a specialist BPO goes about recruiting versus a generalist BPO, who is recruiting for a wide range of roles and doesn't necessarily have a deep understanding of any of them.

If you choose to build an offshore team, this is a *critical part* of the project.

## Advertising

There are two main sources we get our candidates from. One is a website called JobStreet.com. The other source is referrals from existing staff. Other options beyond that are recruitment agencies and less popular websites. We've also tried Facebook advertising, which has yielded limited results.

Because we are trying to fill five to 10 roles each month, and we only hire a small percentage of applicants, it's important to have a reliable source of candidates. JobStreet is still the main place we source candidates from, even though we have to wade through a lot of crap to find the good ones.

When you advertise for a position, you need to understand that most applicants just hit the 'Apply' button. In most cases, they don't read the ad properly. And you will hardly ever get a cover letter. It's just not routine in the Philippines. My opinion is that most applications are very low quality. That's why you need to build a process to eliminate the unsuitable people quickly.

## Filtering

We work through the applications and look primarily at their qualifications and job history. Accounting requires most staff to have a college accounting degree. That eliminates some applicants who have done a course in management accounting or something related. Some of those courses are not eligible to take the CPA board exam in the Philippines, so we tend to stick to Bachelor of Science in Accountancy only. But, as with all things in recruiting, there are exceptions from time to time, depending on a candidate's experience. We also look at people who have an unstable background - job hoppers - and usually eliminate them. If there's something interesting about them, we'll give them a chance to explain, but most of them are struck off the list immediately.

We look at their salary expectations, which are disclosed in JobStreet when they apply. If they are too high for the role they are applying for, they are eliminated. Some people have an overinflated expectation of what they can earn and I can't be bothered to deal with it. I'd rather hire people who are excited about what we offer than negotiate downwards. To this day, I refuse to negotiate salary with anyone. We always make a good offer; they can take it or leave it. I'm very open about this too. We had one girl who applied for a job with us and she asked for a salary that was too high given her experience. I actually contacted her and explained why I couldn't proceed with her application, and how I wouldn't like to disappoint her with a lower offer. She replied saying the salary was negotiable. I told her I wouldn't negotiate but that she was welcome to come and have a chat anyway. Turns out she simply had no idea of the market rates and apologised for this. There was no need for an apology and as her interview was perfect, I offered her a job. For those who know the staff in our business, that was Jesseca. She's now been with us for over three years. She's a senior accountant and in the last two years has trained over 40 other accountants.

Other things we look for in applications are stupid errors. On the rare occasions I've received cover letters, they've sometimes been written to the wrong company. I have seen all sorts of mistakes in applications, but the biggest one is typos. This annoys me so much because a simple spellcheck would find and fix that. But they miss their chance - usually because I feel that if they can't do a spellcheck on a CV then they aren't likely to care much about the quality of their work either.

We eliminate a significant number of applications at the **filtering stage.**

## Invite for interview

The next phase is to invite people who pass our initial screening in for an interview and assessment. This is one of the most frustrating parts of recruitment. We email, call and text candidates to invite them to the office. Many don't respond. I've given up trying to figure out why. As an aside, we also have a number of candidates who just walk into the office unannounced. This is normal in the Philippines, so my team just process them when they come in.

For those who do respond, you can expect only 50 to 70 per cent of them to actually show up for their interview. I'm always looking for ways to optimise our pipeline, so we've surveyed the 'no-shows' to find out why they didn't turn up for their appointment. Common reasons are they forgot or something else came up (or some other bullshit excuse). Again, we've tweaked this to death and the best show up rate you can hope for is about 70 per cent. We even position the interview by telling them on the phone, *"If you can't make it, please call us so we can put someone else in your place."* But many don't bother calling and we never hear from them again.

The upside of this is we get to eliminate another round of unsuitable candidates. And that's the whole point as we go through this process - put enough obstacles in their way and only the best will remain at the end. I know that turning up to an interview you've been invited to attend shouldn't be an obstacle, but it is in the Philippines.

## Assessment day

When an applicant turns up for their interview and assessment, we log their time in a spreadsheet. We are watching them right from the start. If they are late for their interview and didn't inform us they were running behind we send them home. Traffic in Manila is insane, and I understand punctuality can be a challenge if there's an accident or something, but there's no reason for failing to inform us ahead of time – it's simply good manners.

I've gone out of my way in the past to meet a candidate who proceeded to be a no show. Once, I walked through shin-deep water to get to our office for an interview. The girl didn't show up. We called her and she was still in bed. I'm way calmer now than I used to be, but I could have murdered someone that day. Because I was so wet, I did my other interviews that day in rolled up jeans and bare feet. Unconventional, yes, but a great conversation starter!

**The process the candidate goes through in the office involves the following:**

→ Application form

This provides basic personal details, job history and a series of short answer questions. These help us understand the candidate's motivations. They also give us information we can use in the interview to help the conversation.

→ Personality profile

We can see their strengths and weaknesses with this tool. It also helps us direct some interview questions. You can choose any one of the numerous personality profiles on the market - they all basically tell you the same thing.

→ Aptitude test

This covers word meanings, numeracy and logical skills.

→ Essay

We make the candidate write 500 to 750 words telling us what their goals are over the next five years, and what they are willing to do to achieve them. Initially, I created this essay simply to test their English. I've since learned that most applicants have okay English. Some are better than me, but most are just okay – this is good enough for the type of work we do.

We have since discovered that this test is far more useful for filtering out candidates who are not aligned with the direction our business is going in. I've had some candidates write in their essay, *"I want to work at Frontline and within five years move to PWC and become a manager there."* Those candidates aren't getting a job at Frontline!

None of these tests are a deal breaker in themselves (unless they want to work at PWC). We are looking for patterns. If a candidate does a bad interview and a bad test then it's a 'no'. But a candidate might have a weak test score, but perform really well in the interview. That might get them through. There are no hard and fast rules, so use your judgement. Some candidates actually give up and walk out halfway through their assessment, which is good - it saves us time and the hassle of having to make a decision.

→ Interview

This IS the deal breaker. Most candidates fail a basic interview. Usually it's a lack of English. The second main reason is an attitude that doesn't fit our culture.

My personal interview style is **conversational**. I want to get to know the candidate, so I usually talk about anything other than work if I can. I want them to be comfortable. Filipinos can feel intimidated around authority, and if you are doing an interview you are an authority figure to them. So, I usually make fun of myself or anyone else who is nearby. Most of the time I can get the candidate to relax and laugh. I will proceed through their application with them and discuss their previous jobs. In particular, I'm looking for their motivation behind leaving previous companies. Most candidates leave other jobs due to boredom and terrible pay or conditions. This is good to know. If you solve that you can reduce your staff turnover. What I'm looking for are opportunistic types. If they were being paid well but kept changing jobs and seeking more money then the interview is over.

During the interview I specifically ask about any conflict with previous employers and colleagues. I want to know what caused it and how it was resolved. Why? I'm looking for leaders who can deal with problems and I aim to filter out people who cause problems.

I have a *very good* 'Bullshit Detector' too. I can smell it a mile away. As soon as I detect that someone is not being 100% straight with me, I grill them. The receiving end of one of my interrogations is a scary place. It's like being cross-examined by a barrister. I remember one dude who hesitated when I asked him if he was punctual in his last job. I didn't blink - *"Don't bullshit me,"* I said, while staring deeply into his soul, *"I will call your old boss and ask him."* He looked a bit embarrassed and admitted to having some punctuality issues at times.

I'm 100% open with candidates, I expect the same in return.

Punctuality at interviews is an important part of the process. Filipinos aren't known for being good at timekeeping. I'm not particularly interested in cultural norms on this issue - I expect people to turn up on time. If they don't, then I will presume they take a carefree attitude to their work, too.

I had a candidate who was applying for a marketing assistant role. Let's call him Urkel, because that's exactly who he looked like. Urkel was a character from the 1990's sitcom, *Family Matters*. Google him before reading any further if you don't know who I'm talking about. It will help you visualise the interview a bit better.

Urkel was a skilled graphic designer. Nokia and some other big brands in the Philippines used his work. But he turned up late for his interview and didn't tell us ahead of time. He also had business shoes on, pants rolled up past his ankles and wasn't wearing any socks. Apparently that's the thing at the moment. Whether it's trendy or not, I don't really want to hire people who look like idiots. I asked him bluntly, *"Where are your socks, dude? You shouldn't show up for an interview looking like that."*

He didn't have an answer, because there is no answer. He should have worn socks. But I digress.

*"You were late. Did you tell my staff you were running late?"*

*"Umm, no. Sorry."*

I continued with the interview. His skills were a perfect fit...but I had concerns about everything else, so I came up with a solution, as I didn't have any other good candidates at the time. I decided to offer him a role as an independent contractor, rather than an employee. He would receive exactly the same benefits as any other employee, but I wouldn't have the legal obligations if he didn't fit and I had to get rid of him. If he did well over the next six months as a contractor, I'd move him onto the team as an employee.

Urkel was delighted with my offer and was to start work the following Monday morning at 7am. This role reports directly to me, so I bought him a new laptop then spent my whole weekend preparing so his start would be smooth. I turned up at about 5am on the Monday morning so I'd be well on top of things and ready to help my new marketing assistant integrate into the team on his first morning.

Then I waited for him to arrive.

7am came, but my marketing assistant didn't.

So, I waited.

7:15am, but no Urkel.

7:30am, still no Urkel.

One of my staff called him and of course she received the usual bullshit excuse, *"I'm really sorry, I'm stuck in traffic,"* he said.

I had other staff starting that morning too. And they were travelling a lot further to the office than Urkel. They turned up at 6am to make sure they wouldn't be caught in traffic. But Urkel didn't take the role as seriously as the other staff. Remember, I had my doubts about him fitting in, but I gave him a chance even after he was late for his interview.

At 7:45am, Urkel walked in and went to his desk. I was on a Skype call with Jon. I told him to wait a minute, because this wouldn't take long. I walked over to Urkel, told him to come to my office and bring his bag with him. There'd be no need to unpack anything.

Urkel sat down in my office and I told him that turning up 45-minutes late on his first day was unacceptable and I wouldn't be proceeding with our contract. Then I told him to leave.

*"Sir, please. I want to work here. Please give me a second chance."*

*"This WAS your second chance! You were late for your interview and I extended some grace for you and gave you this second opportunity. If this is how you respond to a second chance, then you won't succeed here. You can leave now."*

Urkel started crying, but I was firm. And pissed off. He got up and left. I got back on Skype with Jon, who had listened to the whole thing.

*"Brutal,"* he said.

*"I don't care. I wasted my whole weekend on that clown,"* I replied.

And we moved on and talked about something else. That was the end of Urkel. The upside is that another marketing assistant walked through the door soon after and she is still with us today.

You can imagine how over the course of 1,000+ interviews, I've accumulated enough stories to fill a book. Despite the numerous bad applicants I've had to deal with, I've also had my share of success stories. I'll share some of those with you shortly, but first I want to touch on another important part of recruitment: **Checking references.** Most businesses don't do this very well.

→ Reference checking

We check everyone's references and I do not care for personal ones. I don't want to talk to their best friend or their brother, or anyone else who's likely to only say nice things. The only people we want to talk to for a reference check is their previous supervisors, and preferably at least two or three of them across different employers. This is so we can see patterns of good or bad performance.

We also chase down international references if we can, but that's harder. When we call for references, we always try and call the main landline for a company, not the cell phone of the person we need to talk to. How do we know someone isn't getting their sister to pretend she was the candidate's former supervisor? And we don't usually do email references either. We want to talk to the person.

Back in the early days of our business, we had a candidate who had done a good job through the application and interview process.

He was ready to start working for one of our clients. But we still had to check his references. One of my team spoke to the person he listed as the supervisor on his last job. Clearly that person hadn't been prepped very well because they admitted they weren't his supervisor – just one of his colleagues. And the funniest thing was, that person didn't even try and help. They said straight up the candidate had punctuality issues and was often late for work.

His own friend dropped him in the shit! So I called our client and suggested we withdraw the job offer and find someone else. But our client wanted to proceed and thought the punctuality issues might have just been because he lived a long way from his office. I said, *"But he lied!"* To me, that's a deal breaker. The client really liked him, so we called for another reference. They said the same thing. *"He often turned up late for work,"* they reported. I checked the location, and it was not far from his house. The client agreed at this stage not to proceed. When we informed the candidate he wasn't even surprised.

On the flip side, I rarely receive requests from people for reference checks. Most of our staff remain with us, and most of the ones who leave do so due to performance issues. I have only ever had two or three employers contact me for a reference check on our former staff. And we've probably had a couple of dozen people leave over the years. That means one of two things - either they are lying on their job application and not putting Frontline as a place they've worked, or the other employers are not doing their job properly and checking references.

When I do interviews, I grill candidates in great detail about their employment history. I am all over employment gaps like a lawyer. If I see one, I'll grill them hard. And even more so if I see a six-month gap, or a job that lasted a short while. Most employers offer a six-month probationary period for staff, so if they left at the six-month mark, or they coincidentally have a six-month gap in their history, I question them and do not let it go until I'm satisfied. It can indicate the candidate didn't pass probation. And often there are things they admit to during this cross-examination...err...I mean, gentle questioning. So, be vigilant. Don't assume everything you are seeing is real.

## Success Stories

When I'm recruiting, aside from basic competence, the one thing I'm looking for is desire. Desire to succeed and work for us trumps most shortfalls in a candidate's application. We actually have numerous examples of this in our business, but I'll just highlight a few so you get an idea of the traits to look for in a good candidate.

### Rhen

Rhen was a referral from another employee's mother. I think that's amusing in itself...that the parents of our staff are sending people to come and work at Frontline. I assessed Rhen's application and then interviewed her. Everything was perfect. Her application was good, her experience was good and her interview was good. Referrals are the best because they are almost zero risk. People we know don't send idiots to work for us. And their background isn't in question either.

But things took a turn for the worse for young Rhen. The next step after doing an interview with me was to do an interview on Skype with our client, who was to make the final decision. This is a tough ask for everyone, but it has to be done. Rhen was one of about four or five applicants for this particular role. I figured she'd be in with a good chance. That was until she did her Skype interview.

*It was a disaster!* Rhen got a bad case of stage fright. She could barely speak. And I sat there, helpless. Of course, Rhen didn't get the job with that firm.

After the interviews were finished, I called her into my office to have a chat. I told her I wasn't going to give up on her yet, and I'd give her one more chance with the next client. We always have clients waiting for staff, so it was a matter of her going through another Skype interview with someone else. I told Rhen to go away and practice the interview situation with someone.

Soon after, she came back for another shot. This time it was different. She sat up straight in her chair and her answers were confident, clear and loud enough to be heard. She got a job offer straight after the interview. It was like a different person had taken part in this second interview. But I knew Rhen could do it because she'd already done a one-on-one interview with me.

It turned out that Rhen hadn't taken my words about practising lightly. She'd gone home and gone over an interview scenario with her boyfriend. Rhen had the desire and the willingness to put in some effort, and that got her over the line.

## Mrs X

This example involves some salary discussion, so I'll make the employee anonymous. Mrs X applied to work at Frontline with a few years' experience working in a role that had nothing to do with accounting. Her salary was tracking along okay at the other job, but it was limited and she desperately wanted to work in an accounting firm.

I had a problem, though. Mrs X was seeking a salary that was a step up from where she worked before. Unfortunately, she really only had graduate level skills in accounting. This is a difficult situation for the applicant, and for us. So Mrs X and I had a heart-to-heart. I explained that in order to be employed with us she would have to take a step back before moving forward. I explained her skills were still graduate level, despite her experience in an unrelated role. She understood that she was going to have to take a pay cut so that over the following few years she could power forward with her career and far surpass what she previously earned. I shared my personal story – I graduated from university in my early 30s and then had to accept a graduate-level salary.

I asked her to trust me.

She did.

And over the next three years or so her salary did surpass what she previously earned. I respect people like that. And Mrs X has never forgotten our conversation that day. It comes up sometimes when her salary is increased. And no matter where she goes with her career in the future, I'm glad I was a part of helping her launch it.

### Angelica

Angelica didn't show up for our interview. That's worse than being late. And it's a deal breaker in all cases. The candidate is immediately rejected. But I guess I have a soft spot in my heart somewhere after all. Angelica was a graduate seeking her first job and she had made a mistake with transport times. I personally would have done my research first, but her reason sounded legit. And she was very sorry. So I gave her a second chance. But I didn't make it easy. I told her she had to be in my office by a certain time that day, which meant she had to move quickly to get there. And she did too. Angelica turned up and did a good interview. Of course, I took my opportunity to mock her lack of planning, but I gave her the job anyway.

She still works for us now, so I'm glad I gave her the chance. At first she was very scared of me (no idea why) and would actually run out of my office after picking something up from me. It was hilarious. But things changed as her confidence grew. These days, she mocks my Australian accent, has threatened to punch me and called me a loser after she beat me at darts. That's the kind of working relationship I like! And it's been fun to watch her journey too. In chapter eight of this book, I'm going to talk about how I nearly permanently screwed this up for her.

### Jade

When I graduated and was seeking my first job, I offered to work for free so I could prove myself. In marketing, it's called a 'risk reversal' - I just didn't know it at the time. It was intuitive. I'll take the risk, so there are no barriers to the employer giving me a chance.

I've interviewed over 1,000 people and nobody has ever walked into my office and done the same thing. Can you imagine, as an employer, someone walking in and saying, *"Give me a chance. I don't want a salary, just give me a chance to prove myself and you can pay me later if you think I'm good enough."*

When I tried this, not only did I get the job, but I got paid from day one too. At Frontline, Jade, a friend of mine, came the closest to doing this. She has a substantial call centre background and can even recite the alphabet with a convincing Australian accent. But she had no admin experience and wanted a change in her career. Jade asked me for work experience in admin so she could put it on her CV. At the time I didn't have anything to give her, which frustrated me.

But, sure enough, a job came up soon after. One of our clients needed an admin person. So I put Jade forward. Because I'm transparent to a fault, I explained to the client how she was a friend of mine and had no experience using Microsoft Word or Excel. Even so, they gave her a shot. Jade was given a data entry task to do at home in Excel. She didn't go to bed and instead stayed up the entire night to complete it. And she did a great job too. Jade was hired and has since been promoted and travelled to Australia three times. After only three years her career with us is extremely far removed from her call centre life. Amazing work.

### Von

Von is our IT guy. He worked in the shop that sold us our computers when we first started our business, and I can still recall the first time I met him. The manufacturer had screwed up and packed the wrong cables in the box. I was about to fly back to Australia and had to get this issue sorted before I left. I was having a meltdown. But Von told me not to worry and he'd make sure it was fixed. For some reason, I felt calm and trusted him to sort the problem out.

Von not only fixed that issue, but he went on to work for us as a contractor on the side of his full-time job. And as the business started to grow, we talked to him about joining us full-time. This was a big move, as he'd been working for the shop for a long time. But the salary there was terrible so it didn't take much to persuade him to resign and come and work for us.

Over the years, Von has grown into his role. His English was poor and he needed to develop his technical skills. These days, he can talk to clients on the phone in the UK and Australia, and his skills are significantly better than when I hired him. Von is one of the hardest workers I've come across and I'm also now the godfather of his son.

Von has moved from working on his own managing the IT requirements for about 20 staff, to becoming the IT supervisor for a team of three other IT staff. He's now responsible for the IT needs of over 200 staff across the business. He's also got a few pay rises along the way and jokes with me about how rich he is.

### Mae

Like Jade, Mae is another friend of mine whom we hired. At the time we recruited her she was working in Malaysia. How do you think she did her interview?

Easy.

She got on a plane and came back to Manila just to do it.

We have candidates every single day who can't travel one hour to get to an interview on time, or even show up at all. Mae came from another country.

And because she is also super talented we hired her immediately. And within six months of working for our client, she has been promoted.

## Desire

What's the common thread through each of these stories? I see desire. I see people who really want the job. And people who won't let obstacles get in their way, whether that's stage fright, an ocean, lack of skills or minimal English, each of these employees overcame their difficulties, got hired and succeeded in their role.

There are people like this everywhere. We have lots of them in our business. But they aren't easy to find. We only hire one per cent of applicants, so we have to go through a lot of people to fill a role. And sometimes you have to look carefully at an applicant for signs of desire. It would have been easy to dismiss Rhen's application and move on to the next candidate. But I saw something and didn't let it go. Von could have used English as an excuse, but he didn't. He demonstrated a desire and his whole world has changed for the better.

When you are recruiting, make sure your candidate has the basic skills you need. But the next thing to look for is desire. If they bring that to the table you should be able to train most other skills into them anyway.

In conclusion, if you use a BPO to hire your accounting and admin team, make sure you use a specialist. They will understand your needs more than a generalist, and they will probably have better recruitment processes to cater for a particular market.

If you apply what I've taught you here, you should have a good success rate with the people you hire. Most of our staff are successful. But some are not. No matter how much I try and optimise our recruitment process, there are two things I can't figure out.

Firstly, I have *no idea* which employees I hire will be superstars.

Secondly, some staff can do a good application and interview and the references check out, but then they just *can't do the job*. Given we hire only about one in a hundred applicants, we clearly have a good process for removing unsuitable people from the system, but some still get through. It's rare, but it happens.

So make sure you have your eyes wide open when you hire people and you will save yourself a lot of grief later.

CHAPTER SEVEN

# TASKS AND DAILY ROUTINES FOR AN OFFSHORE TEAM

Naturally, I'm asked about what the offshore team can do. Rather than answer the query with a long list, I tend to take the opposite approach. They can do anything that doesn't require a geographical presence. That means if a physical presence isn't required for a task, then it can be done from the Philippines. You'd be better off making a list of the things you need doing in the UK or Australia - client meetings, scanning and other such things - anything else can be done offshore.

Here's a sample list to get your mind thinking creatively about how you can move some of your tasks to an offshore team.

## Tasks

### Accountants

- Organise and lodge quarterly BAS/IAS
- Year End Compliance for individuals, companies and entities of all types
- Preparation of financial statements
- Workpaper preparation
- Management reporting
- Cash flow forecasting and budgeting

- Bookkeeping
- Technical research
- Payroll preparation
- Invoicing and debtors follow-ups
- Contacting the taxation office/HMRC to resolve queries
- Company incorporations, tax registrations and registrations of other types
- Auditing procedures of various types
- Software setups and implementation
- Client accounting software support and training

## Admin Assistant

- Update weekly newsletter and blog posts (i.e. WordPress)
- Place orders for supplies and promotional products
- Preparation of client letters
- Scan and store receipts/invoices
- Collate and manage financial statements and other critical documents
- Obtain quotes from suppliers
- Carrying out research on particular data, topics (e.g. for presentation purposes) and software products
- Social media monitoring and updates
- Calendar scheduling for meetings and travel
- Basic Microsoft Office tasks (e.g. Spreadsheet creation and updating, PowerPoint presentations)
- Invoice preparation and follow-up
- Creating project plans
- Preparing systems documentation and manuals

- Maintaining the client database
- Managing email campaigns
- Accounting team support (job preparation, finalising and arranging sign off)
- Dealing with government bodies like ASIC and ATO (phone and mail)
- Travel bookings and planning
- UK annual return/confirmation statement filing
- Dealing with UK HMRC regarding client's company & personal taxes

## Marketing Assistant

- Tracking leads' information and details
- Preparing leads reports to track success rates
- Keeping a record of conversations regarding follow-ups with leads. Also provide reminders on when to contact leads.
- Prepare proposals for potential clients
- Support sales by arranging presentations, proposals, videos, brochures, banners, etc., using Adobe Suite programs and CorelDraw
- Collaborate on website design, landing pages and other marketing collaterals, execute what's been agreed and produce material
- Implement, monitor and edit internet ads (e.g. LinkedIn, Facebook)
- Communicate with website contractors or printing suppliers for delivering collaterals correctly and promptly
- Manage email campaigns
- Preparation of newsletters and email series to be sent to clients and leads

- Conceptualisation and execution of company events and celebrations
- Documentation of events and editing of promotional videos
- Respond to client/customer enquiries effectively

## IT Support

- Client remote servers (includes troubleshooting and error repairs)
- SBS backups
- Symantec Backup Exec
- Scheduled server checks of client servers
- Small Business Server 2008, 2011, 2012
- Terminal Servers
- Exchange Server 2007, 2010
- Event log checks for errors (and many more)
- Webhosting checks of client servers
- cPanel checks
- Website Disk checks and management
- Webmail management
- Accounts management (suspended, over-quota)
- Spam checks, bandwidth usage
- Trend antivirus checks of client servers
- Virus and spyware cleaning and management
- License renewal
- Update, component and version upgrades
- Trend seat allocation and acquisition
- Other support

- Auskey troubleshooting
- Remote desktop support via TeamViewer
- CloudHive troubleshooting (and many more)

## Daily Routines

This section is to give you a glimpse into the typical daily routine of the staff. Working in the Philippines is nothing like the UK or Australia. This is because it's a 24-hour country. People are working shifts that serve Asia Pacific, the US and Europe. The country never sleeps.

I'm often asked about how the staff get to work, how they feel about working in the evening and whether they are happy in their jobs, etc. This section is written by them - all I've done is tidy up a bit of grammar. The rest is their words. I've tried to give you a cross section of the business - from accounting staff, to marketing staff, to admin staff, to support staff in our HR department. My business partner has even contributed, so you can see what his day typically looks like working with an offshore team.

### Jon Ryall,

*Director and Founder – Business Advisory, Australia*

I helped launch Frontline in late 2011. I've always been more of the 'technical accountant' guy within the practice and my skills are predominantly around training staff, building good systems, quality review and general business development. My vision has always been to move beyond compliance work and get 'hands on' with clients' businesses to ultimately help improve their value.

At the time of writing this, I manage a team of five Filipino accountants, two personal assistants (also in the Philippines) and an Australian manager doing contract work in Canberra. This is all possible by running the business using cloud software.

My work revolves around supporting my team of accountants with their work, overseeing 'back of house' and making sure clients are happy. I also provide quite a bit of support to our accounting firm clients who are new to offshoring and need tips and ideas to help make it work.

## Morning

After dropping my kids off at school, I usually log on around 9am, which gives me a little time before the offshore team start their day (depending on daylight saving).

Everything is done online. I'll pick my work location based on what client meetings are scheduled that day and whether they are face-to-face, via the phone or online.

I usually know what my team are working on because we catch up for a group meeting at the end of each day. They tell me what is planned for the next day, so that frees me to get on with the things I need to do.

Working remotely can be a juggle between being too accessible and not accessible enough. It's a balance. Having a daily catch-up meeting and setting some ground rules with the Manila team helps keep us all productive.

---

Every three or four months, I like to schedule a four to five day trip to Manila to spend time working directly with my team in the office.

---

## During the day

My work is extremely varied. I could be working on boring tasks like file reviews and sign offs, or more interesting consulting work. From time to time, one of the team gets stuck on a particular technical issue or client problem. My approach to these situations is probably not much different to how you would manage your 'onshore' juniors. I usually push them to 'have a go'. Check Google, look up the legislation, draft a client email (for me to check) and tell me how you intend to solve the issue. Essentially, I'm encouraging staff to think and problem solve, rather than just going into 'processing mode'. In some cases, I also encourage the offshore team to call the client directly (VoIP phones make this a breeze).

## Client meetings

I take the same approach to training my offshore team as I do with my onshore staff. I like to involve them whenever possible. If I have an important meeting over the phone or Skype, I'll invite the staff to be in on the call so they can observe how I deal with clients and the solutions we come up with. There is no issue about this from the clients' end. They understand that my offshore team is doing the work and it saves queries later.

## Working with my accountants

I've already outlined some of the ways I work with my accountants. Overall, the substance isn't a lot different than working with accountants anywhere. When I worked at Deloitte, I had to train my team, review their work, provide feedback and help them plan their career. The staff there respected me because I took a personal interest in them and did my best to provide opportunities for them to grow.

I've found that my offshore team are no different. They have studied hard to get their CPA and generally want to do well with their career. They see working with us as a good opportunity and by providing them with career development, they (mostly) give respect and loyalty in return.

The main difference is *how* the work gets done. I try and provide training as often as possible (like I received at all my accounting firm jobs), but it usually needs to be delivered online. Staff appraisals are also done online, as are our daily workflow meetings. You get the drift.

## Working with my PA

A lot of people like to call offshore assistants Virtual Assistants (VAs). I don't like using this term any more than I like being called a Virtual Accountant! I think the term 'virtual' implies that it's inferior or less value than face-to-face.

Essentially, we all do the same work, whether accounting or admin, but from different locations. In the future, given the prevalence of online work, I think people will call the setup 'multi-office' or 'multi-location' rather than onshore and offshore.

My PA manages my calendar and email, keeps our systems manual updated and is the go-to person for many of the internal communications, whether it's someone chasing me for a phone call or following-up client information requests.

The tasks for accountants are usually fairly obvious, but I've found the tasks a PA can do are only limited by my own creativity. She has arranged flowers for my wife, helped research hosting venues for our quarterly accountants' mastermind groups, managed my personal and work-related travel, and many other things.

Given that my PA's role is less structured than the accounting team, I like to make sure I catch up with her either on the phone or via Skype at least once per day. We just chat about what I'm doing (so she can advise others who are looking for me) and discuss her current projects, any phone calls that need following-up and any client or staff issues I need to deal with.

*By reading through these stories you'll get a good look under the hood of a BPO and their staff.*

### Adhel – Senior Accountant, Australia

'I have been working with Frontline since July 2014. Before joining the company, I was a treasury assistant in a construction company for a year, an auditor in a medium-sized auditing firm for three years and a general accountant in a convenience store for a year. All of my previous employers operate under the Philippine tax system, which is why joining Frontline has really been a great challenge for me. I knew nothing about the Australian tax system, but with the help of the bosses and the cool training they provided, I have been able to learn. They even gave me the Australian Chartered Accountants Module during my first two months in the company.

I do bookkeeping, payroll processing, tax return preparation, activity statement preparation, annual accounts preparation, month end reporting and a bit of corporate secretarial work. I also train the newly hired staff members for our clients who opted for our two-month training programme. During my first six months, I helped build our team's systems manual to help streamline our internal processes.

I ride a jeepney to get to work. I usually arrive at least 30 mins before 7am so that I'll have enough time to grab some breakfast and do my morning routines, such as checking what's new in my Facebook newsfeed. By 7am, I am all set to work. Before I do my job for the day, I clear my emails and see if there's anything urgent that needs to be addressed first. I look for possible tasks that I can give to the trainees to keep them busy for the day. I also assess what jobs I need to prioritise. If I am not sure I ask my boss. Every afternoon we have a daily team huddle with our bosses, wherein we report what we did and what our roadblocks were. I usually go home at around 5pm.

What I like about working for Frontline is that the bosses push me to my limits and there are lots of things to learn, which makes the job even more exciting. When I'm not at work I usually spend time watching movies and TV series, getting massages, reading books and doing a lot of sleeping!'

### Cherry – Operations Manager

'I started at Frontline as an administration assistant in January 2014 and got promoted to office manager after a few months. In 2015, Jon and Mark gave me another round of good news and promoted me again, this time to operations manager. I handle the overall operations of the company, which includes IT, operations, recruitment and HR.

Before Frontline, I worked in the call centre industry for eight years and for more than three years I was a subject matter expert at Intuit QuickBooks. I handled different campaigns and had significant interaction with foreign clients.

I normally wake up at 6am and play with my St. Bernard dog (named Tiny) for a few minutes before I prepare for work. I don't usually eat breakfast but sometimes start my day with bread or something light to eat. I have a flexible schedule because I manage both shifts (Australia and UK), but I make sure I'm in the office at 9am to cover the busiest hour of the morning.

Once I'm in the office, I check with our HR manager and office manager on pending tasks from the previous day. I ask for updates on what we have finished and what tasks still need to be done. I will spend an hour or so getting updates and sorting out any bottlenecks.

*Then I check each room in the office (we have five) to see if everyone is in, if they have any concerns about work, if they have enough work to do, or just to make sure everyone is having an awesome day.*

*Part of my role is to supervise our IT supervisor. I catch up with him every morning and make sure all our internet connections are okay, or if the staff have any computer requirements.*

*I also look after the recruitment team. Every morning I gather them together to give me feedback. I ask them how many applicants confirmed to show up, how many passed, why they did not pass and if they have recommendations to improve our process. I do the final screening before an applicant is endorsed to a client.*

*I spend the rest of my day making sure everything is in order. Every day, Mark catches up with me to keep me up to speed and provide additional instructions. My job is to make his life and our clients' lives easy.*

*Currently, I spend most of my time with HR concerns and mentoring our HR manager and recruitment supervisor. As both of them are new, Mark and I invest time training them and ensuring they get all the support they need. Both of them are superstars so it's easy for me to pass on all my knowledge. Mark wants me to ensure I'm on top of everything. I'm his eyes when he's not around, so I check the staff are aligned with the company's policies. I'm like their mother in the office, so to speak.*

*The best part of my job is when I travel! I have been to Australia several times to meet our clients, and I have been to the United Kingdom six times for conferences and client meetings. This is when my sales skills are being tested. I have been the official ambassadress of Frontline in the UK. Meeting different people, hearing stories about how they started their firms and knowing how Frontline can help them is exciting. Some people we met during those conferences became our clients and friends.*

*I leave the office at 6pm, but sometimes still work from home. I have some clients who will email me even after work. I don't have an off switch so it can be tiring, but it feels great when you've responded to someone and they appreciate what you've done – THAT makes my day!'*

### Jess - Senior Accountant, Australia

*'I have been part of Frontline Accounting since September 2013. I joined the team as a fresh graduate with nine months' experience with a multinational outsourcing company that handled bookkeeping, payroll and corporate secretarial services. I began in client accounting and was transferred to the finance team after a few months.*

*I live with my family in Manila. My travel time from home to office is usually one to two hours.*

*Upon arriving at the office, I clock in and take a look at what jobs I'll be spending my day on, based on what I listed the day before. I also check my inbox in case any urgent stuff came through overnight.*

*We train staff for other firms, so I check what our trainees are planning for the day and give them something to do if they are at a loose end. Then I focus on the job at hand.*

*Today, I'm preparing a month-end management report for the client. I extract the reports and populate them in our tool. I then ask Jon to review the file.*

*A busy day also includes answering client queries (e.g. tax debts, coding accounts into Xero), dealing with questions from the trainees on whatever practice tasks we gave them and reviewing some of the trainees' and teammates' work. I'll ask my colleagues for help whenever I need a fresh set of eyes, or if I'm stuck with something and need a hand.*

*On typical days, I might be doing payroll processing, tax return preparation, sorting out Self-Managed Superannuation Fund (SMSF) administration, conducting lectures for trainees, reviewing Business Activity Statements (BAS), performing weekly bookkeeping, developing training materials and getting on the phone to talk to clients.*

*Almost every day is different. The combined variety and repetition of providing these services gives me the opportunity to learn new things and improve my skillset. My work and my bosses really push me out of my comfort zone to become a better version of myself.*

*After clocking out, I spend some time chatting with my office mates or I catch up on what's trending on social media while waiting for the shuttle home.*

*If it's a game day for my favourite basketball team, I head to the colosseum to cheer my lungs out.*

*Two Wednesday nights of the month are allotted to attend Toastmasters, an organisation that helps people improve their public speaking and communication. Other evenings or weekends are spent catching up with friends or just chilling out at home.'*

### Jandy - Marketing and Admin Assistant, Australia

*'I started at Frontline in 2014. I left my job as a marketing manager with the largest retail store in the Philippines after three years in order to challenge myself. The artist in me refused to be caged. I live for the adventure, so I took a leap of faith*

*and accepted the job as a marketing assistant at Frontline.*

*My first and last interview for the job was with the Big Grumpy White Guy (Mark). I wasn't prepared to have an aneurysm that morning from speaking in English, but I had fun sharing my enthusiasm for marketing with Mark. And what really made me take the job was when he shared his love of books and lent me a marketing book by Jon McCulloch. My heart beamed knowing that Frontline encourages learning and growth.*

### The sunrise

*I wake up around 4:30am to prepare for work. Before I take a bath, I play with my cat and dog for around 10 minutes and feed them. Then I prepare some fruits and milk to take to work. By the time I've bathed and gotten dressed it's around 5:30am. I kiss my mom then get ready to face Manila's traffic head on.*

### The grind

*The first thing I do is check my email before discerning the urgency of each task. I'm a bit forgetful, so I neatly write them down in my notebook. After that, I look back at my previous list and see if I left out any other tasks, which can then be included in the day's list. When I have everything locked and loaded, I'm ready to work.*

*I take care of some administrative tasks, but mostly I work closely with Mark on marketing. We've created the proposal documents and company videos. I help translate what Mark wants Frontline to be as a brand. At times I handle touching base with some clients.*

*I'm usually the main support for our office manager, Sheryl. I make sure she doesn't get swamped in all the office madness. Client and staff comfort is our top priority. They smile, we smile. We make sure there are no hindrances in achieving the highest possible efficiency of workflow with both clients and staff. We don't mind going the extra mile to guarantee Frontline's engine runs smoothly.*

*I also handle all events for the company. Surprise birthdays, summer getaways, Christmas parties, and everything in between. You name it, I can make it happen. This is the part of my job where I can be free to let my creativity run wild – well, not that wild, since Mark's budget isn't as nice as he is!*

### The sunset

*At the end of the day I get to hang back most of the time with some of the teams or Frontline peeps. People in our team are amazing and very fun to be with, but there are times when the grind goes beyond our work hours. This is when we have to hustle big time, but it doesn't matter. After the chaos we always find time to have fun and keep our sanity in place. Working at Frontline is like working with family. There will always be challenging times, but we get through it with support from one another. On top of that, working with family always allows you to be yourself and that's what makes me look forward to another sunrise and the daily grind.'*

### Mae - Personnel Assistant/UK Companies House Specialist

*'My day starts around 11am since I work mid-shift (UK shift - our shift starts at 3:30 PM MNL time) and I live four to five cities away from the office (that's roughly two to two-and-a-half hours travel, with time allotted to traffic). I eat brunch around 11:30am, because that's technically my breakfast and I watch the news to see if the MRT (Metro Rail Transit) is working, as that's my main mode of transportation from work to home.*

*I take a bath, talk to my mom and see to it that I'm out the house by 1-1:30pm.*

*I've been doing this travel routine for about nine months now. I'm just three months away from my first year anniversary with Frontline! Yippee!! You may think it's a bit toxic, but hell no! I've conquered it! As everyone says, I'm a master commuter! I always get into the office 30 minutes or sometimes an hour before my shift. I don't like the feeling of doing a hurdle when going somewhere, whether it's for work or not. This is why I always allocate a lot of time for travelling.*

*I worked abroad before joining Frontline. Yeah, the salary was good, really good. Imagine no salary tax deduction, no everyday traffic dilemma and a whole lot of perks. That's why a lot of people are asking why I moved back to the Philippines when I could have stayed where I was and saved a lot of moolah. I always respond, "If you aspire for career growth you can't be complacent."*

*Frontline used to have one employee in a condo unit and now the number of staff has just passed 200! I've been with companies that are more concerned with the development of the business and totally forget about the welfare and development of the staff.*

*True enough, as I passed probation with Frontline, I was promoted from admin assistant to personnel assistant and I was sent to the UK to meet my bosses. The career move was really fast. That was such an awesome experience.*

*At present, I am doing a transition from my old role to my new one. For the admin role (UK Companies House Specialist), I see to it that all UK clients' annual returns are filed online and on time. I also communicate to clients by email regarding any amendments that need to be done with their returns or any changes of detail that need to be logged on the database. While on the personnel assistant role, I deal with our UK and Philippines staff members' HR needs. While trying to juggle these two roles, I'm also training our newly hired admin assistant. I am teaching her new systems so I can fully take over the role of personnel assistant. In a span of nine months I have learned so much and I'm still learning. Before my day ends, I also ensure that I have zero emails in my inbox. One thing I learned from* working for a BPO company for seven years is how to multitask and manage your time properly.

Now it's time to head home. Same travel time (a bit shorter since it's night time), same route, but now with a sense of fulfilment since a good working day has ended. Normally I get home around 1am. At this time no malls are open, which means no temptations - that's why I can get eight-hours of sleep every day. What is there to complain about with Frontline? Nothing. It's indeed the best place to work.'

### Dianne – Administrative Assistant, UK

'I started at Frontline as the first UK staff member in May 2015. I didn't know what Frontline was - I just heard about it through a friend of mine who happens to be their recruitment specialist (the only one back then). She told me to try my luck with the company.

Before Frontline, I worked for three years at a Korean company as an English tutor-turned-supervisor. The mundane tasks of checking thousands of pages of homework submitted by Korean students and managing around eight to 20 people finally got to me, so I decided to look for a job where I could really grow and learn new things.

Usually, it takes 45-minutes to an hour-and-a-half to get to work, depending on how the traffic is. However, because my UK shift doesn't start until 3:30pm, rushing to work is the least of my worries. I even have the luxury of squeezing a few additional hours of sleep into my morning and extra activities, such as going to the gym near the office and having a late lunch with some of my colleagues.

Unlike in my previous job, my routine at Frontline varies from day-to-day and this keeps me on my toes. It's hard to tell what's in store *for me when I take my seat and check my email.*

*There are days when most of my job involves adding new products onto the company website, managing their website's blog and social media accounts (Facebook, Twitter, LinkedIn and Instagram) and helping put together their monthly newsletter 'Club Row Chronicle'. Sometimes, though, my boss will ask me to do other things, such as helping with his marketing campaigns (which I find very challenging) and promoting his book on social media. Once, he also got me to help put together a company event and a personalised product catalogue for our client.*

*Despite the variety of things I do during my eight hours at work, I always leave the office at 11:30pm and go straight home, where I spend an hour or two reading a book, writing random stuff, watching some videos on the internet or chatting with my fellow night owls (a.k.a. fellow colleagues on the UK shift). Then I go to sleep.*

*A year and four months ago, I had absolutely no idea how to do this job. However, here at Frontline everybody makes sure you have everything you need before subjecting you to any task. They encourage you even when you make mistakes. Thus, I always come to work and tackle each day with confidence and positivity.'*

### Irish - Accountant, UK

*'My previous accountancy jobs in Singapore and Dubai were far different from how I'm working now at Frontline, where I'm an offshore employee of A4G, a UK company.*

*I'll give you just a brief background of how I decided to finally settle in my beloved Philippines. Working abroad has helped me develop my professional skills and grow as a person. Earning a better salary (compared to the local rate), being independent and experiencing new things are just a few of the perks that came with it. During those six years abroad, I had a lot of trying times at work, but I was motivated and looked at it as preparation and training. Then came the time when the everyday routine no longer challenged me and being away from my family didn't make sense anymore. I prayed earnestly for God's leading and He gave me the desire to come back home. So to make the story short, I flew back and trusted God to lead me to the right place...and that is where I am now.*

*I joined Frontline in December 2015. The first few months were a big adjustment because I have to travel for two to three hours just to get to the office. I wasn't used to all the traffic and pollution. Then I had to learn to cope with this new environment, where my colleagues are miles away and the only way of communicating with them is through Skype and emails. What amazes me is how A4G do their business, as every task has a written procedure. Understanding and following these 'systems', as we call them, is a challenge in itself. Aside from that, the ability to follow these systems within the time allocated for each job is very important. The most crucial part of our daily task is completing a timesheet for seven-and-a-half hours each day, detailing each job done. The purpose is to gauge a person's productivity with an individual chargeable target percentage each week. Most of the time I have to extend my working hours (and work on the weekend sometimes) just so I can have a fair, if not excellent, performance.*

*So here goes my typical day at work. My specific job is to prepare the billings. The requests come from all the client managers (accountants) and I have to complete them within two days of the receipt date. Every Monday I also have to complete the time ledger report. This is the summary of time and cost spent by the employees over the week, and it's the basis of the weekly performance evaluation. Whenever my workload is low I do other finance support as well. Asking for work is the best practice because it is easier to complete the timesheet.*

*Coming to work every day is a joy. I consider myself to be part of a team with the people I work with in the UK shift, even though we work for different clients. A friendly and welcoming culture has been established, and this increases as we grow in number - new staff members are joining almost every week. The relationship that we have gives us a good working environment. Jokes and laughter are typical and can be heard constantly throughout the night - it always lightens the mood and helps me cope with stress.*

*I extend my working hours every day, mostly with my A4G colleagues. It's past midnight by the time we leave the office and most of the time we eat out before heading home. We work hard but we do know how to reward ourselves, too.*

*In less than a year at Frontline, I've learned to strive to be productive each day. And I think this sums up one of my life verses, which says, "'Whatever you do, work at it with all your heart, as working for the Lord and not for human masters.'(Col 3:23). I'm always grateful to Frontline for this opportunity."*

# CHAPTER EIGHT

# HOW TO SCREW IT ALL UP

In this chapter, I'm going to share with you some lessons I've learned through client screw-ups and many of my own. Ignore these lessons at your own peril. By the end of this chapter you will know exactly what not to do when building an offshore team.

## Lesson #1: The Classic Train Wreck - A Basket of Problems

Let's start the ball rolling with the biggest offshoring mess I've come across. Most issues I see are fairly narrow and there might just be one or two problems that need to be addressed. In this case, the whole thing was a problem. They had them all.

A manager came to see me a couple of years ago asking for help. He'd recently started working for an Australian accounting firm in their Manila office. And he was concerned. He had written about two pages of notes to bring to our meeting. So we ordered a pizza and went through them while we ate lunch.

The firm had been incorporated about four years earlier. They weren't using a specialist BPO for accountants. In fact, they were not using a BPO at all. They were on their own.

We started working through his list of issues.

**The main problems were:**

- Little to no staff training.

- Work quality was terrible. There were no systems in place for the staff in Manila or Australia.

- The office manager sat at her desk all day with headphones on listening to music. She was supposed to manage about 10 staff in the office. This didn't happen and she had little interaction with the team. Her skillset was around the level of an admin assistant and she was being overpaid by a large margin.

- The attitude of the staff in the office was poor and the team didn't really seem to care about their work.

- The staff weren't showing up for work on time and there was some absenteeism too.

- There was a high staff turnover. Almost nobody lasted more than a year.

- Poor document management.

- Slow turnaround of work (hardly a surprise given all the issues they had).

Things weren't running well. We went through each issue line by line.

*"What should we do?"* the manager asked me.

*"Are there any staff on the team you would keep?"* I asked.

*"None."*

*"Then I would close the office, retrench the staff, find a specialist BPO and start again where your chances of success are almost certain. I don't care if you come to me, or someone else, just find a place that works for you."*

We finished our pizza and the manager went on his way. A couple of months later he got in touch with me to say they had closed the office and that was the end of their journey in the Philippines. The interesting thing was that one of their staff applied to work for me. Needless to say, he didn't get past our initial screening. It's a small world. I've had a few candidates over the years apply to work for me after working for another Aussie I know. They never get hired.

## Lesson #2: The First Person I Sacked - Punctuality Issues

As you've probably realised from the recruitment chapter, I'm tough on punctuality. When people are late I think they are showing a lack of respect for the time of the person on the other side of their appointment. I also think they are showing a lazy attitude that is likely to spill over into their work.

Way back when we were still green when it came to recruitment, Jon and I tried to fill an admin role. We had scheduled several candidates to come to the office for an interview. One of them was running late, much to my frustration. We had been texting back and forth over her being 'on the way' and 'nearly there'. After waiting about 45 minutes, I sent her a text message telling her not to bother, as I wasn't going to wait any longer. And of course the reply was, *"I'm downstairs, I'm here and ready for my interview."*

I spoke to Jon and told him I wouldn't be interviewing this candidate. *"If this is how she treats a job application,"* I said, *"imagine how she'll approach her work if we hire her!"* But Jon is way softer than me, which is why I used to call him Mr Ten Chances. (He's hardened up a bit over the last few years after dealing with so many stupid people).

*"Nah, give her a chance. She might be a good employee,"* he said.

I reluctantly agreed to interview her.

She did a great interview. And as a bonus, she had significant payroll experience. That meant she could do our admin tasks and help our accountant with payroll preparation for our clients. She seemed the perfect fit. Except that she showed up so late for her interview.

So we gave her the job.

*And that was our mistake.*

She was late on her first day. I spoke to her and explained how we couldn't run a business with staff turning up at random times. We needed her to show up on time so we could get our work done in a planned, orderly way.

Then, at the end of her first day, she waited until I was offline (I was working in Australia on this particular week) before sending me an email telling me she'd be late the next day because she had a commitment at her child's school. Instead of 7am, she would get to work at 11am.

She hadn't bothered to ask me during the day if this way okay and she was being manipulative by waiting until she saw me offline. We always let staff put family first, but she would have known ahead of time about this commitment and had chosen not to tell us.

The next day she didn't show up at 11am as promised. She graced us with her presence at about 1pm. Again, I spent time discussing why this wasn't cool, and that I expected her to turn up to work on time from then on.

On day three she turned up on time. I thought we might have turned the corner and things would start to improve.

On day four she was late again. When she got to work, I told her to shut down her computer and leave. She begged for another chance and I just told her to go.

We could have saved ourselves the hassle by not employing someone who shows up 45-minutes late for an interview. My gut told me not to hire her, and any objective view of the situation would have told us not to bother interviewing her in the first place. So, we learned a lesson that remains with us to this day. I made one exception for Urkel (see Chapter Six), but I sacked him in his first five minutes rather than waiting four days.

## Lesson #3: The Second Person I Sacked - Massive Breach of Trust

I trusted our staff. I figured they would always do the right thing, even when I wasn't looking.

*I was wrong.*

Most of them do the right thing when I'm not looking. Not all.

I hired a girl to be my personal assistant/admin assistant for the business. Let's call her Shifty, because it rhymes with her real name. There were red flags all over Shifty.

Shifty's actual application was very good. She's the first person to ever write a personalised covering letter to me. The problem was she lived a long way from the office. I emailed her and said her application was outstanding, but I'd have to decline because of her location.

Her response was exactly what I look for in a candidate (refer back to Chapter Six).

*"My location is not your problem, sir. It's my problem and I'll deal with it. Please give me a chance."*

**Desire.**

So, I gave Shifty a chance. She passed our interview and I gave her the job.

Shifty had spent seven years working in a school before coming to us. She was in an administrative role there, and had very little accountability. On her first day with us, she pulled out her personal laptop and opened it up on her desk next to her work computer. Why would she need a personal computer on her desk while she was working? To chat to her friends of course! And it was right in front of me. I sat there all day getting more and more annoyed as the hours passed. But I had other staff in the room, so I didn't say anything for fear of embarrassing her. I just sent her an email at the end of the day and told her not to bring the laptop to work anymore.

Shifty did an okay job in her first few weeks. Not outstanding, but not a failure either. But as time passed (one to two months), I sensed something wasn't quite right. Remember, Shifty was probably about the third person I'd hired, so I was still feeling my way a bit. I was giving her tasks to do and I noticed the list of things was backing up. Her tasks were not being done. I was puzzled, but didn't worry too much. At that point, I simply trusted her and gave her the benefit of the doubt.

One day, I walked past Shifty's desk and noticed she hit ALT-TAB on her keyboard when she saw me. I knew this changed the screen to something else. She was fast, but not as fast as me.

I knew something was up, so I did some research into computer security. I decided to install keylogging software on her computer, then I sat back and watched. A few weeks later I analysed the results and couldn't believe what I saw.

Shifty had been spending her days talking to some dude in the US. She even opened her webcam so he could watch her work (not that Shifty was doing much work anyway). Creepy stuff. The chat logs were interesting too. He asked her if she was busy and enquired whether her boss would be upset by her sitting there chatting. She told him she wasn't busy and it didn't matter. That solved the mystery as to why she wasn't getting her tasks and projects completed!

I called Jon in Australia and told him what was going on. We had to get rid of Shifty, so I said, *"I sacked the last one, it's your turn this time."*

*"Nah, mate! You are way better at this stuff than me,"* he said.

Damn. I *hated* sacking the first girl - I felt like I had ruined her life. But Jon wasn't going to do it, so I had to. I called Shifty and gave her the good news. She begged for another chance, but I wouldn't budge. I could never trust her again and I would always wonder if she was working or not. She continued to text me for another two to three days asking for a chance. After Shifty left, I gave her tasks to one of my accountants, and she completed the whole lot in a couple of days.

About a week later, I met Shifty for her final salary - and to get my office keys back. I hadn't slept much since it happened. Sacking her was traumatic for me, and just like with the first girl, I felt like I'd ruined Shifty's life. I know it was her fault, but I still felt horrible to be the one to sack her. Shifty walked in and sat down. She was smiling, relaxed and happy. I was still devastated.

*"What's wrong?"* she asked.

Crazy question, I thought. But I told her how I felt about what she'd done.

*"You've done me a huge favour,"* she said. *"When I came to work for you I had bad habits and no accountability from my previous job. You've taught me a huge lesson about the corporate world, which I will take with me for the rest of my life. Thank you."*

She thanked me for sacking her! Shifty had already found another job, so hopefully she went on and kicked some goals elsewhere. Remember my chapter on recruitment and reference checking? Nobody called me. So she either lied about a gap in her CV by telling the new employer she was on holiday, or the employer was careless and didn't bother calling for references.

---

The lesson to take away from Shifty's time with us is that you need to monitor your staff.

---

I don't mean you have to check their computers, but if they aren't getting the work done, it's a sign something else is going on. Manage the workflow and do some digging if something doesn't seem right. We have monitored all the computers since that day. Staff are told on their first day that we do it, and that we check the logs. It's not a secret. But some staff still sit there dicking around chatting to friends. Then they act surprised when we call them out on it.

My stress level when sacking people reduced dramatically the more I did it. It's ALWAYS the employee's fault, and if they want to come and work for me and basically rip me off by not doing their job, then they can leave. I don't really care much anymore when it gets to that point, and I feel relieved when the person is gone.

## Lesson #4: Not Setting Staff up to Succeed

This is a **big one**. For most people, offshoring is new. You need to make sure you set your staff up to succeed. Don't just sit them on a desk and expect them to produce miracles for you. It doesn't work like that. This is even more important if your business is growing fast like ours has.

I'll share with you how I got this wrong in my business and lost one of my own team members.

Angelica came to me as an accounting graduate. It was her first job and she worked on my internal accounting team helping with payroll, month end reporting, government reporting, and other such fun tasks. Trouble was, Angelica started in 2014, when we were out of control. Our senior accountant, Sam, was struggling to get on top of the workload for the team, despite everyone working hard. The girls on this team were routinely doing 15-hour days to get through the work. I wanted them working eight-hour days, but this was a struggle during our growth phase. What happens when the workload is unbearable? Mistakes are made. Angelica was making a lot of errors in her work. And it was annoying me, because I want high quality outcomes. Everyone on the team was pulling long hours and working under stressful conditions. And this went on month after month.

My focus during that time was operations and recruitment. I didn't have the capacity to spend time helping our accountants work out their mess. That was a mistake on *my* part.

The day Angelica gave me her resignation was the day I realised how bad things were for my team. **I had failed as an employer**. I didn't set her up to succeed, and I didn't intervene when she was clearly overworked. It wasn't me driving the team to overwork - that's not what I wanted - it was their choice to do it. We were all doing that.

But Angelica was waking up at night having bad dreams about it. Not cool.

The next day I moved myself into my team's office and mapped out their whole routine on the whiteboard. I did this task by task. We got control of the workload and since that day the stress levels (and the overtime) in the finance team have been lower.

But we lost Angelica and I never felt good about it. She was going to go and take the CPA board exam after leaving Frontline. I offered to pay for it, even though she no longer worked for us. She was stubborn and refused my help. But we always stayed in touch. I remember one Friday night I got a text message from her.

*"How's it going, mate?"* she said, imitating an Aussie greeting.

*"Good. You miss us, don't you?"* I replied.

*"Maybe."*

And sometimes she'd drop over to the office or my condo and say hello. I kept telling her to come back. And, after being gone for about a year, Angelica finally returned to Frontline. And she has done a great job, too. This time she's received a lot of training and support. We put her on Jon's team, set her up to succeed and she has exceeded his expectations.

The lesson here is don't just put people in a job and expect them to produce miracles for you.

There's also a further lesson for you, which is to know what's going on inside your teams. It took me a while to figure this one out, and I still get this wrong from time to time.

# Lessons # 5, 6 & 7: Several Lessons in One Scenario

If you **don't train the staff, monitor their workflow** and **get your local team in Australia or the UK on board,** your offshoring project is probably going to fail.

Let me give you an example of what happens in some BPOs. In our first six months in the Philippines, we used a generalist BPO provider. Our employee was in a room with about 30 other staff. At any point in time, several of them would be asleep, watching videos on YouTube or generally being unproductive. I visited for about 10 days each month and sat there with them.

I caught one of our staff sleeping once. She had her head down on the desk in the middle of the office. I was mad! I woke her up and told her to go to my office. I was about to launch into full-blown Human Resource Disciplinary mode.

*"Why were you sleeping?"* I demanded.

*"Umm, it was my break."*

*"Ahh...shit. Sorry,"* I said sheepishly.

Sometimes I feel like such an idiot.

But my point is, we *know what the staff are doing most of the time.*

Some time back, I sent an email to all the staff and asked them to let me know if their Aussie boss wasn't giving them enough training or work to do. One of the staff replied telling me she was a CPA with four year's experience and our client, her boss, had her doing two hours a day of data entry, and that was it.

For me, that's unacceptable. My team members' careers must be the priority. I called her boss to find out what was going on. It transpired that the partner of the firm was running around winning work and dealing with clients. She wasn't in the office much and her two Australian accountants were hoarding the work and basically ignoring the Filipino staff. Offshoring cannot work under those circumstances and when it emerged the Australian staff didn't want to change the way they worked, we all agreed to end the engagement. I redeployed her Filipino staff to other firms.

If you don't communicate with your teams in the UK and Australia they won't have any buy-in to the offshoring project.

> If you don't train your staff and monitor their workflow, you will have floundering workers in the Philippines sitting around twiddling their thumbs.

You will be wasting your money and they will be wasting their careers.

## Lesson #8: No Relationship With Your Team

Sometimes (not too often, thankfully) I get a question from a prospective client that I find strange.

*"Are the staff loyal to you, or to us?"* they ask me.

*"If you don't act like a dickhead, why would it ever be an issue?"* I usually reply.

In other words, the model works well as it is. The staff are well connected to us in the Philippines and to their employers in Australia or the UK. There never needs to be a question concerning whom they are more loyal to. It just isn't relevant.

That said, I have seen firsthand the difference in the firms who have put in the time and effort to build a relationship with their Filipino staff compared to those who put little, if any, energy into the relationship.

Some firms, not many fortunately, have not taken the time to meet their offshore teams. I can tell you firsthand that the morale on those teams is lower. It's not necessarily a showstopper, but it is healthier if you meet the team face-to-face at some point.

I had a situation once where a client didn't build a good relationship with his Manila employee. I also struggled to work with him, and in the end he made one of my team cry because she made a $27 mistake on an invoice. So I ended the engagement and gave the client the choice to take his business to another BPO.

I never told his employee about my problems with him. I kept it private. That was until he started to badmouth me after I ended the engagement. The employee knows me and we have a good relationship, so she was shocked by what she heard. He was complaining about money and how I was charging too much, and other pedantic things. The employee ended up in tears over it, as she didn't realise what he was like. When she found out the truth she refused to go with her employer and asked to stay at Frontline.

Can you see why you need to build a good working relationship with your staff? You can easily lose employees if you don't.

## Lesson #9: Right Team Members in the Right Roles

It's important to get the right team members in the **right roles**. A couple of years ago, we hired an accountant for one of our clients. She ended up doing a lot of admin work for them rather than accounting.

She wasn't happy, her performance suffered and that meant the client wasn't happy and wanted to end her employment. Something didn't sit well with me, so I got involved to try and help. Normally when I see performance issues, there's a bad attitude that goes with it. We get those people out of the business as quickly as possible. This was different, because the employee's attitude was very good.

I decided to throw her a lifeline. I called the client and suggested I take her off his hands and put her in my team for some training.

Then I suggested he replace her with an admin assistant rather than another accountant. He agreed and thanked me for going to the trouble.

**I sat down with the employee, who assumed she was about to lose her job. I told her I would put her into my own accounting team and one of three things would happen:**

1. She would fail to meet our expectations and her employment would be terminated.

2. She would meet our expectations and be redeployed to another client, but only if I could look the client in the eye and tell them she was good (and the client would receive full disclosure regarding her patchy start with us).

3. She would exceed our expectations and I'd keep her on my team.

We go a long way to ensure people's careers are protected. The employee joined our team and a couple of years later she is still on my team and doing a great job.

Our client replaced her with an admin assistant per our recommendation and she's done a great job and the client is very happy with her.

All it took was matching the right person to the right job.

As a business, we get better and better at this. But you should also be acutely aware of what you expect an employee to do and make sure you *match* their skills and desires with the role you are filling. Don't hire an accountant and then throw data entry work at them for 40 hours a week.

## Lesson #10: Communication Breakdowns

Most niggly issues happen because of communication breakdowns. You say one thing and something different is perceived by the other person. Assumptions are made, people don't talk and clarify things and before you know it you have an issue on your hands to deal with. It's rare we have to deal with serious issues like the ones I've discussed in this chapter; they are the exception rather than the norm. But they are real, and if you aren't careful you can end up with a failed offshoring project.

But most issues still come down to a lack of communication. I've had staff in tears because their Aussie boss used two exclamation marks when emailing them. Crazy!! Aussies are very direct and the Filipino employee receiving that email was scared because she thought her boss was being aggressive. That's how it was perceived.

Most issues arise due to communication problems, and most of those issues are minor things that can needlessly become major if not handled quickly. My job is to help you with that, and my team and me are always on the lookout for problems like this. A couple of times each year, my HR manager and operations manager do one-on-one catch-ups with all the staff. That takes days to get through. I talk to the staff regularly too, and just walk around the office making silly jokes and chatting to them about work. Those casual moments are often when they reveal an issue to me.

You have to do your part, too, and make sure you have a good, safe relationship where the staff will be comfortable opening up to you about any hassles they are having. Hardly any BPO will go to the lengths we do, so make sure you pick a good one then work with them to put out any fires before they become too big to manage.

CHAPTER NINE

# A COMMON OBJECTION: WHAT WILL PEOPLE THINK IF I GO OFFSHORE?

Accountants tend to be a conservative lot, and they worry far too much about what other people think. We could actually write a book just about this topic alone. People in general would be far more satisfied with their lives if they stopped worrying about what everyone else thought and just did what made them happy instead.

I'll break this chapter up into two sections. First, we'll talk about what your **clients might think** if you have an offshore team. Second, and most important, what your **staff might think**. I don't suggest for a second you push forward blindly and ignore people. I'll show you how to manage it so you do what YOU want to do, but don't needlessly alienate people along the way.

## What Will Your Clients Think?

Many firms ask me, *"What will my clients think if I use an offshore team?"* I cringe when I hear this.

*"Who cares what they think,"* I tell them. *"Whose business is it, yours or theirs?"*

*"But they might not be happy if their work is being done by staff overseas…"*

Business owners asking these questions are coming at it from the wrong direction. It's *your* business - and the clients need to fit into

Offshore or DIE!

your way of doing things. The client should **not** be dictating to you how you run your business.

**You need to understand that there are several things at play here.**

- ✓ **Firstly, it's your business and you need to run it in a way that makes you happy.** If you want to use an offshore team, then go right ahead and do it. If you want to stop wearing suits and ties to meetings and put on jeans instead then do it. I wear jeans to almost all my meetings, and I can assure you it doesn't negatively affect sales at all. I think it makes me more relatable, more real. I no longer even own a suit.

- ✓ **Secondly, if you have strong positioning you will repel clients who don't want to fit into your way of doing things.** Perfect! Having bad clients is worse than having no clients at all. At least if you have no clients then you can go out and find ideal clients instead of wasting your time with the crap ones.

- ✓ **Finally, strong positioning makes you more attractive than other businesses to your ideal client.** They will see you differently than a business that is easily pushed around. There's a mutual respect - it's a team effort, not a supplier/customer relationship.

Isn't that a perfect recipe for having a client list full of business owners who appreciate what you do and don't bitch and moan and give you headaches?

I'll let you in on a secret. Jon and I didn't agree wholeheartedly at first regarding how to approach the question of, *"Do we tell clients about our offshore team or not?"*

My position was: *"Who cares what anyone thinks? If they have an issue with the way we run our accounting firm then they can go to the firm up the road instead."*

Jon was a bit more reserved, but he came around to my way of thinking fairly quickly.

182

Here's the interesting thing.

When I did sales visits for our accounting firm, I expected I would get pushback on the offshore model. I figured a few prospective clients would have an issue with it at least.

*I was wrong.*

After five years, I have never had a business take issue with the offshore model. Not one. *Ever.* Business owners, in my experience, couldn't care less where and how their accounting work is being done. They just want good value for the money they are spending with you.

In fact, when our first accountant, Cherry, came to Australia to do some tax training, a bunch of our clients she was doing work for came out to have dinner with her and meet her face-to-face. They wanted to show their appreciation for what she had done for their businesses.

If you are bold and if you are confident in your position, then I suggest you take a similar approach. If you ensure your clients are receiving good value from your service, I doubt you'll have any issues. **Communicate with them.** Talk to them. Write to them.

> If you are transparent and show why the offshore team is going to help them, I don't see why you should have any problems.

Now, I understand not everyone is going to feel that way. So, my diluted version of the strong approach would be to segment your client list. Choose the clients who are likely to be most open to having work done by an offshore team. And choose clients who are already comfortable with using cloud-based tools - the modern, forward-thinking business owners. Then start small and gradually have your offshore staff take over their accounting.

Bit by bit, as the evidence grows within your practice that the model is viable and valuable, you will be able to expand across many more of your clients. Maybe you won't get 100% of your clients taking up cloud accounting and being comfortable with offshore staff, but I bet a good proportion of them will be. And if they aren't I'd seriously look at the quality of your client base.

## What Will Your Staff Think?

I mostly work with the partners of accounting firms. They are the ones who first talk to me about offshoring, and they are the ones who get excited and make the decision to hire a team in the Philippines.

But what about the staff in the UK or Australia? How do they feel?

There are several things they might be feeling.

1. They might fear for their job, thinking they could be retrenched in favour of cheaper staff offshore.
2. They might fear the change and how it will impact the comfortable routine they have become accustomed to.

3. **They might be uncomfortable with the idea they have to talk to someone in another country.**

4. **They might not be happy about training someone in another country via tools like Skype.**

5. **They might be excited about having help in the Philippines.**

6. **And finally, they might be indifferent to the whole thing.**

I've seen ALL of those responses from employees in Australia. And that's why if you are a partner reading this, you must *communicate openly and honestly with your staff*. If you don't, you're inviting niggly little problems into your business that can grow into bigger ones and cause your offshoring project to fail.

Another one of our Australian clients had some initial teething problems getting buy-in from their local staff. They were negative about the offshoring project. But this attitude was reversed as each employee spent time in the Philippines with the offshore team. They went back to Australia as fans of the model, and some of them didn't want to go home at all because they had so much fun working in our Manila office.

If your staff are worried about losing their jobs, you can assure them it's not an issue. Every firm we've taken on as a client has come to us for help with growing their practice. Nobody has lost a job in Australia or the UK because of an offshore team. It's about growth, not redundancy. Sure, if there's natural attrition in Australia or the UK then a replacement is sometimes filled in the Philippines, but that's just further proof the model works.

So, in the end it's up to you to be the leader in your firm.

You need to lead your clients and you need to lead your staff.

Opening communication and sharing the benefits regarding having a team in the Philippines to help you is key. If your leadership skills are weak then you might struggle to get your clients and staff engaged with this new model. The good news is that if you are reading this and don't yet have an offshore team, you can look for guidance from the dozens of other firms who have succeeded over the last few years. We've collectively made the path easy to follow for firms just starting out now.

# CHAPTER TEN

# CHANGING LIVES THROUGH OUTREACH

This chapter is not about business and it's not about building teams. It's not about accounting, either. It's about one thing only - **helping people.** If you build a business and make money at any cost along the way, what's the point? Is that the legacy you want?

For some people, it is. It starts and ends with profit and the '*What's in it for me?*' question. That's not how I roll. And it's not how the people in my world roll either. If we see someone who needs help, then we jump in and help. We do prioritise profit - otherwise there is no business - but we don't do it at any cost.

If you grew up in Australia or the UK, you've probably never seen real poverty. And poverty isn't, *"My welfare payment isn't enough to buy my cigarettes this week. Life is so unfair."* Unless you have a mental illness, it's very hard to starve in Australia. There is so much welfare that you can live a reasonable life if you want to.

A trip to the Philippines is an eye-opener when it comes to seeing how some people live. There is a huge gap between the rich and the poor.

If you get sick and have no money, you will die.

The life expectancy of an Aussie is 83 years, the life expectancy of a Brit is 81 years and the life expectancy of a Filipino is 68 years (see Wikipedia).

Jon and I have always been involved in some sort of outreach, even before our Frontline days. About 15 years ago, I worked full-time doing outreach work for kids. I did that for a year, and I still know some of the kids to this day. One of them even tracked me down a few years ago and messaged me on Facebook. I hadn't seen her since she was about 10 years old. Now she's an adult with a child of her own. I asked her why she'd been looking for me and her reply blew me away. *"I've been looking for you for years,"* she said. *"I've never forgotten you and the difference you made in my life when I was younger."* Wow!

**So I ask you:** *what footprint are you leaving in the world? What does your legacy look like?* For me, I want to be the dude who helped people. I want to help business owners build better businesses. I want to help staff develop and achieve their career and personal goals. And I want to help people who are unable to help themselves. The interesting part of this is that I may never witness the difference any of my efforts have made. And like the friend whom I helped when she was younger, if I do it might be many years on.

Our first outreach efforts in the Philippines were an accident. We were trying to help an employee after her house was damaged by a typhoon. She asked us to direct the funds to her community instead. One thing led to another and we ended up spending a lot of time doing outreach in 2013.

To try and obtain further exposure and assistance from our peers, I submitted an entry for a community service award. We didn't win, but we were finalists. I have included that submission over the page, so you can see what was happening behind the scenes of our accounting practice.

*<Start of award submission>*

# Name of Company: Frontline Accounting

## Category Title: Community Contribution by an Accounting Business

This is an interesting award to try and win. Part of me dislikes 'bragging' about the good charitable works we have done and would prefer to operate in secret. I'm happy to brag about business growth, but not charity.

That said, if we are fortunate enough to win this award, it may end up leading to more assistance via increased awareness in our networks and the wider public.

**The summary:**

- I (Mark) personally spent around two months of my year dedicated to disaster relief work in the Philippines.
- Our staff spent many days helping to purchase, pack and distribute relief goods.
- We closed the office at one point and took our team to go and help victims.
- We donated many hundreds of food parcels and water and hygiene kits.
- Hundreds of pairs of thongs (that's flip flops for the UK readers!) were provided for kids with no footwear.
- Dozens of kids received school supplies.
- Hospital treatment was given to a sick old lady.
- We personally funded multiple flights around the Philippines so we were helping at the coalface of major disasters in different areas.
- We provided mattresses for kids sleeping on the dirt, because their home had no floor. The homes looked like a garden shed in the UK or Australia.
- The leftover donations are now putting two kids through a full college scholarship in accounting.

## A closer look at the work we did:

The easiest way to break this down is to explain each outreach we did.

### Cavite Flood – September, 2013

Cavite is an economically depressed area just south of Manila. In fact, if you have been to the Philippines you fly right over it coming into the airport.

One of our employees was affected by a severe flood in that area. Her home was damaged so we offered to fix it for her. She asked us to help her community with the money instead.

We agreed, as long as we controlled the money. The Philippines is a very corrupt country and donating money anywhere is risky.

I have personally never been in a flood, but what I saw was shocking.

The streets were filled with rubbish, furniture and household items that had been ruined, along with endless mud as far as you could see. There was even a coffin that had washed up from the local cemetery and gone onto the highway.

In the first house I went to I found a 72-year-old lady on a 'bed'.

You can't really call it a bed because there was no mattress or pillow. It was a piece of wood. She was in so much pain that she was unable to stand up without help. Her foot was infected due to some disease the rats had spread in the water (I can't remember what this is called).

I promised to come and get her after the food had been distributed and take her to hospital. A few hours later we came back and transferred her to a private hospital where she was tested (she has diabetes too) and given various meds, pain relief and other items.

On the worst day of the flood, the woman had been standing neck deep in water. She had eight kids, 20 grandchildren and was clearly as tough as nails. She'd been sitting there for several days waiting for someone to help her, but no help came. She actually thought I must be running for a political office there due to the random act of kindness we showed her. Strangers generally don't just turn up to your house and get you to a hospital.

On another occasion, I gave a child a mattress to sleep on. His 'house' had six to eight kids (I can't remember exactly now) and two adults living in it. There was no running water or a toilet.

*(Incidentally, the team were very popular with the kids. I'm sure it had something to do with the chocolate we handed out.)*

I went deep into the slums. Here I had to cross a wooden plank to get access to where hundreds of people were living. My team thought I was nuts going in there.

I used to be a bouncer before my accounting days. My old skills were needed to get the crowd off me here. I was buried behind all those people. It was crazy!

This house had no power. I could hardly see anything. The floors were still soaked from the flood and it was no better than a cave. It is lit up on this photo simply from the flash of the camera.

There was a mess everywhere. Things were smashed and broken. Rubbish was piled up all over the place.

This was the outreach where we closed our office and our staff came to help distribute goods to the flood victims.

While I can break down the things we distributed – quite frankly I think a picture tells a thousand words. You can see the large quantity of goods we donated throughout the photos on our Facebook albums. Just look for Frontline Accounting's page and you'll find the outreach albums.

## Bohol Outreach

Bohol is an island paradise south of Manila and about an hour or so flight time away. In October 2013, it was hit by a magnitude 7.2 earthquake.

Shortly after that, they were hit by one of the worst typhoons ever recorded. This killed around 6,000 people in the Philippines. That's a double dose of tragedy in a short space of time.

We organised some friends and they organised a truck.

*Game on.*

We flew down there for one day and handed food and water to approximately 360 people.

We used money that was left over from the Cavite floods. These were funds donated by Frontline, our friends, peers and clients.

Just like the flood earlier, I have never seen with my own eyes the effect of an earthquake. Large slabs of concrete were broken, houses were folded over and people every-where were living in tents. It was simply devastating.

Because the day moved so fast, I didn't really get a lot of photos on this trip.

Here I am with the local mayor.

Below is the line of people that had been standing in the sun for a couple

of hours waiting for our arrival. The mayor in the photo above had excellent crowd control skills! He organised everything.

This is the truck we filled with food and water. We had an awesome team to help us.

Then we stood and handed out the goods to the people in that community. One guy kept me sheltered from the sun. It was a really hot day and my pale face can burn very fast!

*The full album is available on our Facebook page.*

## Capiz Outreach

Typhoon Yolanda was so devastating that we ended up doing several trips to the region.

Capiz is an area that was directly in the path of the typhoon. We have close friends who live nearby.

The father of one of the directors of our Filipino company was in a car that was overturned by the storm and he ended up in hospital.

We flew to Iloilo then drove a couple of hours up to Capiz. It was another one-day trip to deliver hygiene kits, food (freshly cooked!) and water to over 100 people. I can't recall the exact number, as it was another busy day.

The kids here really loved getting their pic taken with the crazy white guy. This never happens in Australia!

This is me and my girlfriend and her aunt. We found her in the city there. She lost her home in the typhoon. Unfortunately, she passed away a few months later.

Driving to this area was like a war zone. Trees, houses and power lines were down for miles. If buildings survived, they often had no roof left.

*Here are a series of pics that were typical of the day.*

## Iloilo Outreach

This was another day trip where we flew south for about an hour then handed out cooked food and other essentials to people affected by Typhoon Yolanda.

My son from Australia was able to come on this trip, which made it very special. It was nice to see him mix with the local people and see what real poverty looks like. Not being able to pay one's phone bill (his normal world) is not 'poverty'!

Here is the local mayor giving me a gift for coming. What an unbelievable group of people. They are smashed by a natural disaster, yet still think of giving me a present for helping out.

Mayor is not the exact description for this man. He's actually the Barangay Captain, but it's like being a mayor of that district.

This man's shirt is a cracker. It translates as *'Hunk'*! My own shirt says, *'My father is Filipino'*, so it made for a funny conversation between the two of us.

*Below is a photo of my boy helping out.*

*Crowds of people were waiting here for us too.*

## College Scholarships

We still had funds left after all the outreaches listed above, so we set about using them to put two kids through a full college scholarship in accounting.

Our staff approached the local high schools and we got lists of kids who were high performers, but in financial difficulty. They needed to want to do accounting in college.

This process took many weeks.

We screened applications and interviewed families. We also visited their homes to ensure they were indeed living in depressed conditions, and that the money would be used by those who most needed it.

Both girls we sponsored came from economic conditions you couldn't imagine. One of them lived in a room with several family members. The bed space, toilet and kitchen were all in the one room.

### Conclusion

It was a really big few months. It was hard work and took significant time and financial resources.

Most Australians will never understand what real poverty looks like.

Hopefully, we can win this award and raise our profile for the next time we do outreach programmes like this.

*<End of award submission>*

So, that was 2013 and part of 2014.

**What have we done since?**

Well, things didn't work out so well with our scholarship programme. We put weeks of work into finding and vetting the recipients of the funds. Unfortunately, both girls ended up failing subjects and dropping out of their accounting course. I was not impressed and swore I'd never do another scholarship again.

Well, we are doing one, but he's a five year old. One of our staff passed away from cancer at just 27 years of age, leaving behind a wife and a young son. So we passed the hat around again, and between staff, clients and us, we can put the boy through several years of school.

After the scholarship efforts, we formalised things a bit more. We decided to ask staff if they wanted to donate part of their salary to outreach, and then we would go out and help people once a quarter. About 85% of staff donated to that fund, along with Frontline and some of our clients.

We visited an orphanage and gave out food, clothing, toys and nappies. We also went to a nursing home. That was like a horror movie coming to life. It's nothing like what you see in Australia.

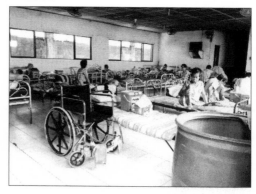

Some old ladies were locked in a room with concrete floors and bars like a prison cell. They slept on beds that had no mattresses and I saw a rat almost the size of a small cat walk through one room. I've never seen anything that big, even on TV.

Most of them had nappies on and were just lying on a bed in a room with a couple of dozen other people waiting to die. They were completely neglected by the outside world.

The upside was they thought I was Jesus. Seriously. The ones with the mental problems were the most fun to hang out with. And now they've met Jesus. How much better could their day get?

While these quarterly outreaches were helpful to the community, they were a huge burden on my team, who had to organise everything. And because my team are the priority, I made the heartbreaking decision to cancel the programme and refund the staff's recent donations.

But my break from outreach only lasted about six months.

I saw a need and couldn't stand by and do nothing. So we launched a staff welfare fund. Staff, clients and Frontline donate to it and it helps them in times of personal emergencies.

**Here are two emails I received after the fund was used to help an employee's father with heart surgery.**

*'Hi Mark,*

*I would like to say a huge THANK YOU for helping me get the money I need for my father's operation.*

*It really meant so much. Earlier, I literally cried in secret because of my happiness.*

*I will never ever forget your generosity. I was so happy and it made me realise that Frontline is different from other companies I've been with. I will be good in my job and will do my very best.*

*I found another home here and it seems like I have another mom (Cherry) and dad (Mark) – hahaha (just kidding).*

*I will give you an update on my father's operation soon.*

*Thank you so much again! God bless Frontline.'*

**And following this email, I received one from her boss in Australia.**

*'Mark,*

*To be honest I was a bit lost for words.*

*We joined the staff medical fund donations because it was a chance to give back to the families of Frontline.*

*I was not expecting that it would directly impact on our staff, as we only have four out of 200.*

*Reading the email was the highlight of my week/month.*

*To know we have been able to help our staff in Manila in a way we would never in Australia is very satisfying. And that's ignoring any business upside.*

*I can't believe there would be any Australian/UK employers not contributing to the fund.*

*I would request that, with permission, you send this email and our employee's email to those not contributing and tell them to get on board and not think it will never impact them.*

*I can see why you jump out of bed every morning and are so motivated at Frontline.*

*Don't stop what you are doing. EVER!!!'*

Responses from staff and clients like that drive me to do what we do. Running a sustainable business is our first priority. We are not a charity, and our business must be strong and profitable. But along the way, we will not ignore things that most people will turn a blind eye to. We roll up our sleeves and do something about it.

That's the legacy I want to be remembered for. And if you set up a team in the Philippines, I'd encourage you to educate yourself on what's happening there and help out when needed. Don't approach it with your Australian or British mindset and assume the government will handle things. They won't. I can assure you the Filipinos live under circumstances that would crush a lot of privileged westerners.

# CONCLUSION

The future accounting firm will not look like the accounting firm of the past. In fact, a lot of accounting firms of today look nothing like firms of the past, including our own.

The challenge you face as an accountant is **taking action** on the concepts I've discussed in this book. Accountants are not famous for being excellent at implementing revolutionary new ideas, but I can assure you that it's not that hard.

I've watched the industry change in Australia. In fact, Jon and I were at the forefront of it. We took things that looked obvious and didn't sit there suffering 'paralysis from analysis'. We did some basic due diligence then had a go. We assessed the risk of an offshore team as very low. If it didn't work, we'd lose about $10,000 and six months of time in trying. If it did work, we could build a unique firm that was future-proof while delivering amazing outcomes for clients.

Five years later, the results are in and we were spot on with our strategy. We have since watched many other firms do the same thing. Some have done it independently and some have jumped on board with us and joined us in our journey.

The end result is that we're prepared for an industry that is going to be shaken up in the years to come. Clients will no longer pay high fees for an accountant to sit there and push a button.

Our accounting firm won't suffer from any of these problems. We have always provided value-added work for our clients, and by using an offshore team we are able to deliver far more value than any firm in Australia or the UK.

I've watched the Australian market evolve over the last five years. The rate of change is breathtaking. After two years of visiting the UK every couple of months, I've now seen the concepts take hold there, too. But it's only just beginning. Some firms still have their heads buried firmly in the sand. That's okay, the smarter ones are putting their heads up, taking a look around and realising they'd better take charge of their firm's future.

What will happen over the next five to 10 years?

Offshore labour and technology will drive the production of accounting work. And onshore staff had better be prepared to deliver a lot more value than clicking a button and lodging someone's tax return.

**The firm of the future will need to Offshore or Die.**

Game on.

# NEXT STEPS:
# SETTING YOU UP FOR SUCCESS

This book contains all the information you need to make your offshoring journey a successful one. It's just a matter of taking action. Most accountants are good thinkers but terrible doers.

> If you have staffing issues in your firm then it would be wise to explore alternatives, such as an offshore team.

If you would like to find out whether this model is a good fit for your firm, email me at **mark@frontlineaccounting.com.au** and I'll give you a hand.

We don't work with all firms who approach us, which is why our success rate is so high. If I can't help you, I will still point you in the right direction.

## My winning tips on how to choose a BPO provider

Every couple of months, I'm approached by a business that has taken on an offshore team in the Philippines but is unhappy with the BPO and wants help moving its team somewhere else.

It's far better to get the choice right in the first place.

**If I was setting up a team of accounting and admin staff, these are the questions I'd ask, in no particular order.**

→ Do you get along with the management team? You will be working closely with management and if you don't like them the journey is going to be a hassle.

→ Does the BPO talk straight? You don't want to have to try and figure out if they are telling you the truth or not.

→ Are they specialists in the accounting industry?

→ Do they have a significant track record of success with other accounting firms?

→ Is the BPO happy for you to speak to their other clients?

→ Is the BPO happy for you to speak to some of the staff about their experience working there?

→ Do they help teach you the processes and strategies to successfully engage, train and manage an offshore team?

→ Are the staff in the BPO happy?

→ Is staff and client turnover low?

→ Are they transparent and do they share with you examples of failures as well as successes?

→ Do they have a track record of rolling their sleeves up and diving in the trenches to help clients and staff when challenges arise?

→ Are they based in an area (such as Manila) where there is an abundance of qualified candidates to work for you?

→ Does the BPO run events where there is a chance for you to meet other clients of the BPO and collaborate?

→ Does the BPO proactively manage the salary levels of staff?

→ Does the BPO proactively manage performance appraisals of the staff?

→ An added bonus would be if the people who run the BPO have real world experience of working in your industry. For example, we not only run a BPO, but we still run our own chartered accounting firm. But that's just a bonus, it's not a deal-breaker.

There are going to be many more things you can add to this list. I'd say that if you can establish the BPO's competency, their management practices are honest and transparent (most over promise and under deliver) and you like them, then that's probably most of the battle won.

*Good luck with your research.*

As I said earlier, if you need some help - or just have some questions regarding an offshore model - get in touch. **Email me at mark@frontlineaccounting.com.au**

*I'll help you get you started.*

# ABOUT THE AUTHOR

Mark co-founded Frontline Accounting in 2011 and launched a BPO service in the Philippines for other firms in 2014. He is a chartered accountant by trade, although he hasn't practised accounting for nearly three years since the BPO business took off. He leaves that to his more capable business partner, Jon Ryall.

Mark spends most of his time talking to people. He loves talking to his staff and helping them develop personally and professionally. He also loves talking to accounting firms and seeing them realise the opportunities in the Philippines for the first time. But if you put more than about three people in the room with Mark, he gets very uncomfortable. He is an introvert, but only those closest to him know this. You will usually find him in the corner at any social event (if he shows up at all), unless his unsympathetic team force him into the spotlight.

Mark spends most of his time travelling between the UK, the Philippines and Australia. He makes about five trips to the UK and about five trips to Australia each year. He racks up frequent flyer miles like nobody you've ever seen. In the Philippines, he has a St Bernard who loves to drool all over him when he gets home from one of his trips. He also lives with his girlfriend and two maids, who make his life run like a well-oiled machine.

Most firms who work with Mark ask him how big he wants his business to grow. Mark's answer is simple. If he's happy, he'll keep going. If he's not happy, he won't. And because of that he removes unsuitable clients and staff from his life. Life is too short for bullshit.

# ACKNOWLEDGEMENTS

Firstly, I want to thank my long-suffering business partner, Jon Ryall for his support. The longer we work together, the better our relationship gets. We understand each other's quirks and working styles, and we ensure that grace and forgiveness is prioritised when we get it wrong. Thanks mate. The last five years have been a blast. I'm a little bit terrified about what we might produce in the next five years after the mischief we caused our industry in our first five!

I also want to thank my Monday afternoon Skype buddies, Mo and Vicky. We get together each week almost without fail, share our wins and losses and basically help each other out in our respective journeys. You guys are both 100% awesome.

Next, I want to thank our clients. It's never felt like a supplier/customer relationship. We are picky about who gets in as a client, and as a result we mostly end up with a good bunch of people going in the same direction as us. It's a big team effort. I appreciate your patience when things go wrong and I appreciate your encouragement when things go right.

Last, but certainly not least, I want to thank our staff. Without you, there would be no business. You are the reason I get up in the morning. Watching you succeed in your careers is like watching my own kids succeed. Your encouragement energises me to keep going when I am tired or wondering what the hell I've gotten myself into by starting this business.